BETTER SEX

The erotic education you never had

BETTER SEX

The erotic education you never had

GLENN WILSON &
CHRIS McLAUGHLIN

BLOOMSBURY

First published 1995 by Bloomsbury Publishing Plc, 2 Soho Square, London W1V 6HB

British Library Cataloguing in Publication Data
A CIP record for this book is available from the British Library

ISBN 0 7475 2048 8

10 9 8 7 6 5 4 3 2 1

Typeset by Hewer Text Composition Services, Edinburgh
Printed in Britain by Clays Ltd, St Ives Plc

CONTENTS

CHAPTER 1

WHAT HAPPENS WHEN YOU HAVE SEX?

Not too long ago, sex was something you did in the dark and never talked about. As the veil of secrecy has lifted, and people have started to discuss their sex lives openly, it's clear that lots of them have problems. It seems that there are four main problems which are very common and cause a lot of upset:

- Women (mostly) who have difficulty becoming aroused ('turned on') or are so uninterested in sex that they try to avoid situations where their partner may make sexual demands on them.
- Women (mostly) who can't reach orgasm easily or, in some cases, at all.
- Men who have trouble getting an erection or keeping it for very long.
- Men who have an orgasm much more quickly than they or their partners want – known as premature ejaculation.

Some of these difficulties may have purely physical causes, but the vast majority have their roots in the individual's mind, and sometimes in problems between the couple. Even when there are no fundamental problems, it's not unusual for an element of routine – or even boredom – to creep into your sex life when you've been together for a long time. The feeling that sex has become more of a habit than anything else is certainly not conducive to an exciting love life, but the worst thing you can do is keep quiet and simply accept the situation as inevitable. The good news is that, however serious and deep-seated you feel your difficulties may be, the chances are very good that you will be able to overcome them given enthusiasm and the right information. These problems and others like them can now be treated effectively, thanks to the research which has revealed so much about what actually happens when we have sex.

The first big discoveries came back in 1966, when the well-known American sex researchers Masters and Johnson published their book called *Human Sexual Response*. Believe it or not, their findings were based on studying more than 10,000 orgasms under laboratory conditions! The scientists used various methods of monitoring the volunteers – among them a dildo-shaped camera which was designed to excite the woman sexually, while at the same time filming the changes taking place inside her vagina.

These observations enabled Masters and Johnson to describe in great detail what happens to men's and women's bodies while they are having sex. They measured all kinds of physical changes that happen during and after sex including heart rate, blood pressure, alteration in breathing and changes in the blood supply to various parts of the body. What they discovered is that certain things occur in a particular order in everyone – with parallel reactions in men and women. What's more, it made remarkably little difference whether the orgasm was the result of masturbation or intercourse – much the same pattern of physiological changes was observed. The researchers named this pattern 'the response cycle', and divided it up into four distinct phases.

1 The excitement phase

You may become sexually aroused by any stimulus which seems erotic to you. It may be touch, but it could also be looking at someone or something, what you're hearing, or even just your imagination and fantasy. As you start to get excited, the tissues in your genital area become engorged. Just how long this process takes will vary, not just from one person to another but also according to circumstances. It's also true to say that, as a general rule, it takes longer in a woman than in a man. While a man may be excited by the mere sight of a nude woman, a woman

more often needs some touching and caressing before she can begin to respond.
SHE: When a woman becomes aroused, her vagina becomes moist and lubricated, certain changes take place in her clitoris and labia, her breasts swell and her nipples become erect.
HE: A man will get an erection, and his nipples may become erect as well.

2 Plateau phase

There are more changes in your genital area, reflecting increases in the blood supply to the region and greater muscle tension.
SHE: The outer part of a woman's vagina swells, which has the effect of making it grip more tightly round the penis, while the inner part balloons out. Her clitoris gets shorter, and retracts so that direct contact with the penis is more difficult. It is so sensitive that friction from the penis could otherwise be painful.
HE: A man's testicles expand in size by about 50 per cent and are pulled up high into the scrotum.

3 Orgasm

When you are actually having a climax, the excitement is at such a peak that you lose all voluntary control of your body for a few seconds. Your heart rate shoots up – sometimes to as much as 180 beats a minute – your blood pressure rises and you breathe very fast. At the same time, you will experience strong contractions in the muscles of your neck, arms, back and bottom, although you may not be conscious of them. Your skin takes on a pink flush, and your face is likely to be contorted. Many people can't stop themselves crying out or moaning in ecstasy – a woman is particularly likely to do this; a man is more inclined to grunt aggressively.
SHE: During her climax, a woman will experience rhythmic

contractions in the outer part of her vagina, her uterus and sometimes in the anal sphincter muscles as well. It used to be thought that these contractions helped to suck the seminal fluid up into the uterus to encourage conception. We now know that this isn't so, however, because the contractions come from the top downwards, as they do in labour. Hence they have no real function in women.

HE: During the man's climax, his penis contracts at the same rate as the woman's vagina, shooting the seminal fluid from his urethral opening at the tip of the penis under considerable pressure. In normal intercourse, the semen is deposited at the inner end of the vagina, close to the cervix.

4 Resolution

This covers the period after sex when your body gradually returns to its normal state. When you've had an orgasm, it can happen quite quickly, and you feel a great sense of release and tranquillity. Some people just feel like falling asleep, while others feel relaxed but alert.

SHE: If her partner continues to stimulate her, a woman can have another orgasm – or more than one – during this phase.

HE: A man will need a certain period of time to recover before he can become aroused again. Exactly how long this takes will vary from one individual to another, and be influenced by factors such as age, fitness, how often he's had sex lately, whether sex with this partner is still a novelty and how desirable he finds her. Men are much more likely than women to succumb to a 'post-coital slumber' – in other words, fall asleep – which is especially irritating to the woman if she herself has not had a climax.

IT'S THE CLITORIS THAT COUNTS . . .

Masters and Johnson gave a boost to women's sex lives by destroying an old myth. Before they did their research, many people believed that there were two different kinds of female orgasm:

- Clitoral orgasm, often brought about by masturbation, which was somehow not quite 'the real thing'.
- Vaginal orgasm, which only happened as the result of friction from a man's penis inside her, and which was supposed to be preferable.

In fact, the findings from their St Louis research laboratory showed that there was no difference, physiologically speaking, between the two. Whenever you as a woman have an orgasm, it is always a response to your clitoris being stimulated. Of course, this can happen in all kinds of different ways, although simple intercourse in the missionary position is actually one of the least efficient. Hand stimulation – either with your own hand or your partner's – or oral sex are much more likely to be exciting and pleasurable and to result in an orgasm. You may well find, however, that you get more pleasure if your partner doesn't try to stimulate your clitoris directly. If he rubs and strokes the surrounding area, it will produce more pleasant sensations in the clitoris than direct stimulation which can even be painful. When he has his penis inside you, the thrusting movements will move the clitoral hood across the top of the clitoris without necessarily being in direct contact with the most sensitive part, so intercourse also provides some degree of clitoral stimulation, albeit an insufficient amount to enable some women to enjoy orgasm.

Like many of the women studied by Masters and Johnson, you probably already take account of this when you masturbate, touching the labia nearby rather than the clitoris, to achieve the same sort of feelings you get when your partner is moving his penis inside you. Some of the other interesting discoveries made by Masters and Johnson might be more surprising, however.

DID YOU KNOW?

Check your sexpertise in our mini quiz – answers overleaf, but don't cheat!

1 *Which gives you a more intense orgasm – masturbation or sexual intercourse?*

2 *Does a bigger penis make for a bigger orgasm for the woman?*

3 *Does it make a difference to either partner if the man is circumcised?*

4 *Does a woman go off sexual intercourse during her period?*

5 *Can sex during pregnancy harm a woman or her baby?*

ANSWERS

1 The researchers found little or no difference in intensity – if anything, orgasms during masturbation seemed to have a slight edge in the intensity stakes. As a woman, you may well reach orgasm more easily this way than through sexual intercourse.

2 Penis size is irrelevant – and that's official. Two factors are important here. First, erect penises vary much less in size than limp ones because the smaller they are, the more they expand when erect. Second, the vagina is good at adjusting itself to fit around the penis, so that the amount of friction will be the same regardless of penis size. According to Masters and Johnson, the dimensions of the man's penis have nothing much to do with the amount of enjoyment or satisfaction you and your partner derive from sex.

3 Circumcision is irrelevant too since it doesn't appear to affect the sexual response of you or your partner.

4 The answer to this depends on the individual. If you as a woman have very painful periods or a heavy flow, you might not feel much like sex, but there is no physiological reason why you shouldn't enjoy sex if you want to. Many women do like having sex at this time, especially during the second half of their period.

5 If you suffer from unexplained bleeding or a threatened miscarriage, your doctor may well advise you to avoid sexual

intercourse and orgasm until things settle down. Otherwise, there is no reason at all why you shouldn't have sex whenever you like. Indeed, many women find they become aroused more easily and have orgasms more often when they are pregnant. There is no way that sex can harm the woman or her baby, with one major exception. A man should never blow air into his partner's vagina because of the risk of causing an embolism (bubble of air), but this is particularly dangerous during pregnancy. Obviously, it is also unwise for the man to pound heavily on top of the belly of a mother-to-be in the later stages of pregnancy. Other than this, though, you can enjoy yourselves as much as you like, knowing that your growing baby is safe and secure inside his or her amniotic sac.

WHAT CAN GO WRONG

What we have been talking about so far is the way things work when your sex life is going well and your minds and bodies are happily in tune. You'd be very lucky indeed, though, if things went that well for you all the time. The number of couples who have sexual difficulties at some point in their relationship is quite staggering. When you're trying to deal with a problem of this kind, it's all too easy to feel as though your situation is unique and that no one else can possibly understand what you're going through. The truth is that what the experts call 'sexual dysfunction' is very common. Whatever your particular problem, other people have experienced something similar, and most of them have come through it, with or without outside help.

THE 10 MOST COMMON PROBLEMS

HE	
What the experts call it:	**What it means:**
Primary impotence	You have never been able to have sexual intercourse because you can't get an erection at all or you can't get hard enough to put your penis inside your partner's vagina.
Secondary impotence	Although you have been able to have an erection in the past, you are currently having difficulty and can't get – or stay – hard enough to have sex.
Situational impotence	You find that getting and keeping an erection is impossible in some circumstances but not others. For example, you may be able to make love with your mistress but not with your wife.
Premature ejaculation	You usually can't stop yourself coming well before your partner has had long enough to reach her climax. Some men actually ejaculate before they have had time to put their penis inside their partner, and a few do so even before they have an erection.
Ejaculatory incompetence	You have no difficulty getting and keeping an erection or with entering your partner, but you are unable to ejaculate no matter how long you go on. This disability is relatively rare.

SHE	
What the experts call it:	**What it means:**
Dyspareunia	Having sexual intercourse is difficult, if not impossible, because it is so painful. This problem is much more common in women, but men also can suffer from it occasionally.
Primary orgasmic dysfunction	You have never actually experienced an orgasm, either when having sexual intercourse or through masturbation.
Situational orgasmic dysfunction	Whether you have an orgasm seems to vary depending on the circumstances in which you are making love. For example, you may find you can climax easily when you're on holiday, but never at home. You may be able to climax with masturbation but not if your partner is present.
Vaginismus	Whenever you try to have intercourse, your vaginal opening clamps itself shut so it is impossible for your partner to get his penis inside. These contractions affect the whole outer part of your vagina, and you seem to have no control over them.
HE or SHE	
Disorders of arousal or desire	One of the partners never or hardly ever feels like making love or just isn't interested in sex at all. Excessive desire, or what is sometimes called nymphomania in women or the 'Don Juan syndrome' (sex addiction) in men may also come under this heading, although fewer people complain to therapists of these problems.

HEARTS AND MINDS

Once they realised just how common sexual problems like these are, Masters and Johnson turned their attention to possible causes. Although the people concerned often thought there must be some physical problem at the root of their difficulty – a hormone imbalance, for example – the researchers found that this was not the explanation in the majority of cases. The real cause was much more likely to be psychological – something amiss either within the relationship, or in the individual's own attitudes or way of thinking.

Careful medical examination of their patients rarely turned up any anatomical or physiological impediment to having sex – in other words, they could find no reason why the patients' bodies shouldn't work perfectly normally and follow the usual pattern of sexual response. A man who was apparently impotent would have erections while asleep, for instance, while a woman who seemed uninterested in sex could enjoy erotic dreams.

There were some exceptions, where a particular illness or other physical factor was playing a part in disrupting the person's sex life. For example, conditions such as urethritis (inflammation of the urine channel inside the penis), diabetes or multiple sclerosis could hamper sexual performance. Other influences which could temporarily affect the ability to make love included tiredness, drinking too much or taking certain drugs, but this sort of problem didn't turn up all that often. Having ruled out a specifically 'medical' explanation, there had to be some reason to account for people's very real sexual difficulties. In the majority of cases, this turned out to be something in the person's background or psychological make-up.

Sometimes this would be something quite deep-rooted, such as a strict religious upbringing which instilled the idea that all sex was dirty or sinful, unpleasant experiences in childhood, such as sexual abuse, an unrecognised preference for homosexual or lesbian sex, and so on. Those individuals with very complex psychological problems might well need treatment or counselling over a relatively long period in order to help them deal with their past and sort out their feelings. For many others – in fact, the majority of those with sexual difficulties – a direct approach aimed at altering their behaviour in the here and now was more beneficial.

CHANGING BEHAVIOUR

In the light of Masters' and Johnson's findings about normal sexual response, most sex therapists today use what is known as a behavioural approach. This concentrates on the specific difficulty a couple is having, helping them to recognise what lies behind the problem in order to overcome it. This may mean looking at certain aspects of the relationship between the two people concerned or examining long-standing habits or attitudes which are interfering with sexual performance. How this works will become clearer as we go on to consider particular difficulties in the following chapters.

When your sexual difficulties are very long-standing or the causes particularly complex, you may need this kind of therapy to help sort it all out. Otherwise, you may be one of the very many couples who can manage on their own without bringing in the experts. Perhaps the most important step you can take towards resolving your problem is to acknowledge it openly – yet this can actually be the most difficult step of all.

There are all sorts of possible reasons for this:

- It could be, for instance, that only one of you realises that there is a problem. A man who has never been able to give his partner much pleasure because he comes too quickly could easily be quite unaware of her feelings unless she tells him.
- You could both realise all too well that your sex life is seriously lacking but be too embarrassed or find it too awkward to talk about.
- One of you has tried to bring the problem up for discussion, only for the whole thing to degenerate into a screaming match where you blame each other and so nothing is resolved.
- Sometimes, sexual difficulties really only exist because they reflect some other kind of difficulty between the two of you. For example, a man may refuse to make any effort to please his partner sexually as a way of punishing her for an affair, or perhaps you both carry your rows and disagreements into the bedroom and use sex as a weapon in your ongoing battle.
- Although your relationship is still good, your sex life has become rather humdrum, and neither of you wants to be the first to suggest spicing it up a bit for fear of being laughed at or rejected.

There are many variations on these common themes, and as many ways of solving the problems once you face up to them. Although some of the suggestions in the following chapters are based on the kinds of treatments offered by sex therapists, we hope that you will actually enjoy experimenting with a number of them. Sex is important, but it doesn't always have to be serious. Quite the opposite, in fact – a shared sense of humour is one of the most attractive assets you can bring to your love life. After all, making love should be a pleasure, not a duty, and there's absolutely no reason why you shouldn't enjoy yourselves as much as you can.

CHAPTER 2

NOT IN THE MOOD?

Most people can't turn sexual desire on and off like a tap, however much they would like to be able to. There will always be times when one of you feels like making love and the other doesn't. Provided it doesn't happen too often, it isn't a real problem. A sympathetic and understanding partner will simply accept the disappointment, and look forward to the next occasion when you both want sex. It's only if that 'next time' doesn't come along very often that you need to find ways of changing the situation. There may be practical reasons which account for your feelings – it's difficult, for example, to summon any enthusiasm for sex if you're tired out, worried about money or not feeling very well. Sometimes, however, not wanting to make love with your partner can be a sign that something is wrong between you or that your relationship needs some sorting out. Only you can work out what factors might be operating in your particular situation, but the questions below point to some of the more common ones.

HAVE YOU LOST THAT LOVING FEELING?

Do you still fancy your partner?

If your partner's original appeal for you was based a lot on looks, then changes like putting on weight, neglecting personal grooming or whatever could be turning you off. And remember that this works both ways – could it be that you take far less trouble to appear attractive than you used to as well? None of us can hold back the inevitable effects of aging on our looks. Our skin inevitably loses some smoothness and elasticity, hair gets drier and less glossy, and may cover ever smaller areas of a man's head. None of these changes need matter much between a loving couple and you can't do much about them anyway, but you can still make the most of yourself. It's not that you're trying to look like a film star, but taking trouble over your appearance is one way of showing your partner that you still care about looking good for him or her. And it is equally important to attend to personal hygiene – it's only good manners to bathe and clean your teeth before lovemaking. If your partner neglects to do this, set an example very conspicuously or invite them directly to join you in your ablutions.

Are you angry with your partner?

Resentment can build up over big or small things and sour your feelings. It might be something important, like the fact that you're not getting much attention or affection, or something relatively small but irritating, such as never getting round to some household chore they have promised to do. The worst thing you can do is to bottle up your feelings because they will be reflected in your attitude towards your partner, without him or her knowing why. When you allow this kind of barrier to build up, it's almost impossible to retain any sense of closeness or intimacy between you, and this is bound to have an adverse effect on your love life. Although you may never have a row or even argue, you get so used to hiding your emotions that you can almost forget you have any. Friends and family are often surprised when a couple like this actually splits up, because they always seemed to get on well together. In fact, the easygoing atmosphere wasn't actually a sign of compatibility, but resulted from the fact that each had ceased to care much about what the other did or felt. If you think your relationship could be drifting in this way, you need to confront the situation before it's too late. Your sex life won't get better until you really start to communicate with each other and re-establish the intimacy you once had.

Has sex become boring?

There's nothing very exciting about a Saturday night bedtime routine that never varies, lasts about five minutes and seems to lack all real meaning. It's not surprising if you prefer to go straight to sleep. This doesn't mean buying a copy of the *Kama Sutra* and working your way through every position, but a touch of spice would certainly help to revive your sexual tastebuds. For more ideas on this, see chapters 7 and 8.

Has the balance of your relationship shifted?

Sometimes, the 'personality match' between a couple which originally worked well is disrupted, leaving one or other uncomfortable with the new situation. Perhaps one partner has changed, becoming more assertive or less confident, or there may have been external changes, such as one partner losing their job, earning a lot more than the other or gaining increased status at work. For example, you may have chosen your partner originally partly because he was extravert and outgoing, while you were shy. Over the years, you have developed more self-confidence, and do not depend on him so much when you're with other people. So the roles which you each played in the relationship may need to change, and you both have to recognise this and adapt accordingly. Similarly, a man whose partner once had a serious weight problem may have been secretly pleased that this seemed to make her less desirable to other men. If she then diets successfully and starts attracting admiring glances – or more –

from other men, he may feel threatened and feel that the changes in her could put their relationship at risk.

Do you feel emotionally threatened?

An affair or even the suspicion that your partner is attracted to someone else can destroy your self-confidence, or leave you feeling jealous and insecure. The imaginary presence of this third party in bed with you is bound to dampen your desire for sex with your partner or eradicate it completely. What you do about this depends on whether the threat is real or imaginary. There's no doubt that jealousy is a very destructive emotion, and can sometimes end up driving the other person away when they originally had no intention of straying. If you can bring yourself to realise that your fears have no real foundation, you may be able to handle your jealousy, but this isn't always easy in practice. If you can't make any progress alone, it's worth thinking about counselling as the reasons for your insecurity are probably buried somewhere in your past, and a trained outsider could help you to come to terms with them. On the other hand, it is often difficult to forgive and forget when you know your partner has had an affair, however much you may want to. Provided he or she has definitely left the illicit relationship behind, you have to try and accept that it happened, that it's over now and that you only add to your troubles by dwelling on it. It does take time to rebuild trust, but when that's what you both want to do, it is possible in the end.

FACING FACTS

Recognising your own situation is the first step to finding a way out of your difficulties. The next step is likely to take longer and involve a good deal of effort on both your parts. You may find that you can't resolve things on your own and feel that a 'neutral' outsider could help you sort out your conflicts. Many couples have found the service offered by Relate (see page 180) was the right thing for them, but such counselling is much more likely to work if both partners are willing to go along to the sessions. When your problems are less deep-rooted, however, talking to your partner about how you feel may be enough to improve the situation, even if your relationship isn't transformed overnight!

Once you've made up your mind to try and tackle whatever relationship problem you think is behind the droop in your sex life, bear the following guidelines in mind:

- Hurling abuse and blaming each other isn't likely to lead to better mutual understanding. However hard it is, try and keep the temperature down, and remember to do your share of listening as well as talking. Sometimes it can help to create an artificial structure for your discussion. For example, you could agree that you will take it in turns to speak, each having the floor for a certain amount of time – say 10 minutes – during which the other one will not interrupt. At the end of the first 10 minutes, you have 'equal time' to reply and give your response, concentrating on the points your partner has made. Then the roles are reversed, so each of you gets the chance to air your grievances, knowing that you will get a hearing and some feedback at the end. When the atmosphere has been soured by a long period of discontent or resentment, you'll probably need several such sessions to clear the air. You might not find this rather laboured approach as satisfying as a good row, but it is much more likely to bring about change and compromise in the end.

- Try to frame your comments in what the experts call 'I language'. This means saying 'I feel I'm not attractive to you any more when I see you eyeing up other people', instead of 'You make me mad when . . . etc.' Or 'I always found that short hairstyle and the way you used to dress really sexy,' rather than 'You've put on weight and let yourself go – no wonder I don't fancy you any more.' This is a way of showing that you are taking responsibility for your own feelings and reactions, rather than blaming your partner and putting the onus on them to improve. If your partner doesn't feel directly under attack, he or she will be less likely to go on the defensive or to hit back at you. At the same time, having to make the effort to express yourself in this way will force you to focus clearly on exactly what your feelings are – whether you're hurt, annoyed, upset, jealous or whatever, and why.
- Whenever possible, it is best to frame your complaint in the form of a positive request or constructive suggestion for change. For example, 'I would love it if you could spend more time caressing and teasing me before we actually have intercourse', or 'I would feel so much closer to you if you occasionally helped me with the washing-up'. Statements such as these are usually much better received than moans, and are much more likely to be effective than accusations and recriminations.
- Be honest about what's really bothering you. You can't expect your partner to read your mind, and he or she

may be quite willing to try and lose those little habits that irritate you so much once you've brought them out into the open. Unless you are conducting some kind of undeclared guerilla warfare, chances are that your partner isn't upsetting or infuriating you deliberately. It's much more likely that he or she is simply unaware of how the behaviour is affecting you, so it's up to you to speak out. When you're angry about something, explain what it is, why you are angry and what you would like your partner to do about it. It's always better to be as specific as you can so that your partner knows what he or she is being asked to respond to. All-purpose moaning is unlikely to get you any further forward.

- Accept that improving the situation may well involve you in change or compromise as well as your partner. For example, spicing up those boring five-minute bedtime encounters is something to work out together – it takes two to make sex more exciting and original.

THAT'S LIFE

For many couples whose relationship is basically OK, it's just everyday life that gets in the way of good sex. You'd be doing fine if you were living on a sun-drenched island with no particular demands on your time, no money worries and feeling relaxed and carefree. As things are, however, real life can take a lot out of you. Juggling all the demands made on you by work and/or household chores, family and just keeping your head above water may leave you with little time or energy for sex. By the time you do get to bed, all you want to do is sink into oblivion for a few hours before you have to face the next day's onslaught.

If this is happening to you, you need to sit down with your partner and try to work out how to change the situation. These are some of the aspects to consider:

- Does your life really have to be so pressurised?
- Can you rearrange the household routine or cut out some of the unnecessary jobs?
- Do you allow other people to pressurise you into things you'd rather not do?
- Do you need outside advice on sorting out your finances?
- Have you unconsciously allowed sex to slip down to the bottom of your list of priorities?

In answering these questions, you're trying to find a way to relieve the pressure and make time for the two of you as a couple: time to yourselves, when you can begin to rebuild your love life and give it the whole of your attention, at least for a few hours. Sometimes this will mean buying the time you need at the expense of other people – letting the cricket team manage without you, cancelling social arrangements that are more of a habit than a pleasure, getting someone else to drive the kids to the swimming pool for a change, or just taking the phone off the hook or turning on the answering machine for a few hours. Those affected may be a bit miffed at first, but they'll get used to it and in any case, you need to make your relationship your first priority for a while.

Having cleared the decks of some of the clutter, you both now have to remind yourselves that making love isn't just something you fit in when you have a bit of spare time and energy. You will probably have to make a conscious effort to change your attitude at first. Don't worry if it feels a bit silly to start with when you make a date to be with your partner the way you did when you first met. Then you probably thought nothing of dropping everything else to see one another because it was all so new and exciting. You can probably still remember how you felt then, so why not see whether you can't recreate that atmosphere and set the scene for a revitalised love life.

GETTING IT TOGETHER

Making time to be together as a couple free of outside distractions is a first step, but it doesn't guarantee by itself that you will immediately want to make love. You almost certainly won't feel like it unless you're relaxed, so give yourselves time to calm down and get rid of any tensions. For some, a good meal with wine or even champagne is the best way to achieve this. Other possibilities are sharing a bath, a slow massage with lightly scented oil or watching a romantic video. The point is that you're concentrating completely on just being together, without outside distractions, and simply enjoying each other's company and closeness. If you do find that you're in the mood to make love, don't automatically retire to the bedroom unless you want to. Many couples find that making love somewhere different, like on the sofa, in the shower or on a rug in front of the fire, provides an element of novelty that helps do away with any boredom.

According to a recent national newspaper survey, sexy magazines or videos are a good turn-on for very many people. These days, you don't have to sneak guiltily into a shady sex shop to find this kind of thing. You will find a good selection of sexy films or sex education videos available in ordinary shops, as well as lots of titillating magazines and books. There's a greater awareness now that many people don't want traditional style porn, consisting of crude genital close-ups, women with unnaturally large breasts or posed anatomical photos of simulated sex. Research has shown that women especially are more likely to respond to erotic material which includes an element of characterisation and plot as well as the sexual encounters. Once you have found the type of material which appeals to you, you and your partner can build up your own private 'library' to enjoy together as part of your revitalised sex life.

IT'S BEEN A LONG TIME . . .

You may feel that, although there's nothing fundamentally wrong with your relationship, it has gone a bit stale. Life together has become rather humdrum and routine, to the extent where you don't really notice each other as people any more. It's not surprising if this complacency is reflected in your sex life – making love is just one more habit you've fallen into (or out of) and has no particular meaning or enjoyment about it.

Restoring the sparkle will take a bit of effort from both of you, and may well mean breaking patterns of behaviour that you've both got used to and taken for granted. Asking yourself the following questions will help pinpoint how things have changed between you:

- When was the last time you really talked to each other about something that matters to both of you?

- When was the last time you spent a really fun or romantic evening out together?
- Do you ever notice one another's appearance – new clothes, a change in hairstyle or a loss of weight, for instance?
- When was the last time either of you made an effort to look good for the other?
- Do you still look forward to seeing your partner at the end of the day, or plan to have time alone together?

Too many negative responses from either or both of you suggests your relationship is seriously in need of some tender loving care. It's often said that women need some degree of emotional involvement before they can enjoy sex and in general that's probably true. What is less commonly recognised, however, is that men frequently find sex more enjoyable and satisfying with a woman who offers them more than a desirable body. Warmth and closeness, and the feeling that your partner loves you for yourself, despite all your faults, is one of the best aphrodisiacs around. Making time for one another and taking the trouble to show that you care will pay big dividends in everyday life as well as in bed.

You need to recognise what has happened between you, and make a joint effort to find your way back to how things used to be. Try talking about the early days of your relationship, reminding each other of things you did and said and what attracted you to each other in the first place. You probably had more enthusiasm for sex back then – reminiscing about past highlights in your sex life may help recapture the old excitement. Rediscovering the person you originally fell in love with is a good way to start building a new and closer relationship.

Recapturing your partner's interest – and resurrecting your own – is the first step to reclaiming your sex life. As well as concentrating on other aspects of your life together, however, you will probably also want to put in a bit more effort than you've been doing recently into the way you look and dress. A word of warning though: it's probably wise not to change your ways too dramatically overnight. If you rush out to buy a whole stack of sexy underwear or suddenly start using lashings of aftershave or perfume, your partner will probably just think you're having an affair!

SETTING THE SCENE

While you may not want your bedroom to look like something out of *The Arabian Nights*, it is worth giving a bit of thought to creating the right kind of atmosphere. You'll be surprised at how easy it is to transform a rather boring bedroom into something that is more inviting.

Getting the privacy you need can be a real problem when you have young children. Unfortunately, you can never be certain that your toddler won't choose the crucial moment to come stumbling into your bedroom for comfort. The very possibility can make it difficult to relax. There may be times when you can make the most of having the place to yourself, or even arrange the occasional night away if your child is happy to be with family or friends. Otherwise, it's a case of doing what you can to prevent interruptions, even though it may not always work. If you know your child usually sleeps for a couple of hours without waking, for example, why not take advantage of this rather than waiting until your usual bedtime to make love? Bear in mind that you were lovers before you were parents and use your imagination to make the most of the opportunities given to you. Even if you do have to accept that you're not always able to make love just when you feel like it, remind yourselves that this stage won't last forever.

- Candles or soft-coloured bedside lamps (a hint of pink or peach works wonders for your skin!) are much sexier than a bright overhead light and don't cost a fortune. The short, stubby, scented candles are preferable to tall ones, which are more likely to tip over and may even start a fire.
- Next time you're buying bedding, what about going for something a bit more exotic than pastel-coloured polyester/cotton? Black satin is not everyone's taste, but a deeper shade or a more slippery texture may be more suggestive and reflect your new sexier attitude too. Duvets are less confining than tightly tucked-in blankets.
- The British climate being what it is, it's good if you can arrange for some means of heating the room quickly so you aren't put off disappearing upstairs because you know it will be freezing.
- If you know (or suspect) that your bed is more than ten years old, it's time to consider buying a new one or at least a new mattress if your finances will stretch to it. Unless your sleeping habits are dramatically different or antisocial, a double bed will do more for your sex life than two single ones. The bigger the better, money and space permitting, so there's less likelihood of one of you falling out when things get passionate. There is no bigger turn-off than a creaking bed-base – if necessary, put your mattress on the floor to avoid this source of self-consciousness.
- Unless you can be certain that no one but you will ever venture into your bedroom, you could consider having a lockable cupboard or drawer to store sexy magazines,

books, videos and sex toys with which you might want to fuel your imagination.

- The last thing you want to worry about when you're having a good time in the bedroom is someone walking in on you. So if there's any chance of that, a bolt or lock on the door will put your mind at rest. Even better, arrange to be alone in the house together for special lovemaking sessions.
- A little background music to suit your tastes is often helpful, preferably not so intrusive or compelling that you stop what you're doing to listen. A radio station such as Classic FM is better than tapes, records and CDs, unless you have some kind of automated changing system to ensure continuity of sound and freedom from interruption.

When you've gone to some trouble to create a warm and loving atmosphere in your room, it's best not to spoil the intimacy by using it for more mundane purposes like sewing or doing the household accounts. You want it to become your haven where the rest of the world can't intrude so it's nice if it can stay as private as possible. Of course, none of these precautions will be much use unless the two of you also try to leave your day-to-day concerns on the threshhold as well. It's worth developing the habit of keeping all your trivial arguments and differences on the other side of the bedroom door. With the minimum of outside distractions to disturb you, you can focus on putting right whatever is in the way of you and a more satisfying sex life . . .

CHAPTER 3

WHEN YOU CAN'T COME

Not being able to reach a climax during intercourse is one of the main reasons why people go to see sex therapists. In fact, this kind of difficulty is so common among women that it could almost be described as normal. Research asking women about their experience of orgasm has shown that about one third say they never or hardly ever come while having sexual intercourse, while another third only come sometimes. It's worth pointing out, though, that many women don't actually see this as a problem – which may be a surprise to most men. As a woman, you may well enjoy sex with your partner and find it very satisfying even though you never or hardly ever have an orgasm. If so, don't allow yourself to be persuaded that you have a problem.

On the other hand, you may be one of those women who would like to be able to come, or feel frustrated when you don't. Or, possibly, you would simply like to know what all the fuss is about. Often, the difficulty is confined to actual sexual intercourse – a woman who can't reach a climax while her partner is inside her may be able to come through masturbation. This might mean only when she stimulates herself, when she or her partner uses a vibrator, or when her partner brings her off with his hand or tongue. For some women the situation is even more complicated – they are able to reach a climax with one man but not another. For example, there may be no problem with a casual partner, even though orgasm remains elusive with her husband or regular partner. None of these problems is likely to be insoluble, but they will need to be tackled in slightly different ways.

A QUESTION OF TIMING

For most men, orgasm is a relatively simple and straightforward business. Given enough of the right kind of stimulation, they will inevitably reach a climax – often sooner rather than later. Because orgasm is accompanied by ejaculation of seminal fluid, it is a biologically necessary process – this is the way the egg gets fertilised. For a woman, the situation isn't the same. She can conceive without experiencing an orgasm; in fact, biologically speaking, she doesn't have to want or enjoy sexual intercourse at all! Looking at it from this point of view, you can see that if a woman often had her orgasm well before the man was ready, then just wanted to turn over and go to sleep, her chances of conceiving would be considerably reduced. In evolutionary terms, this arrangement would be a lot less effective than guaranteeing the man's orgasm, and thus his ejaculation, virtually every time he has intercourse. This leads some experts to believe that while orgasm is a natural culmination of sex for a man, a woman may have to learn how to achieve it.

She is unlikely to get the chance to do this if sex always goes at the rate preferred by her partner. As a woman, the time it takes you to become sexually aroused is much longer, and the amount of stimulation you need to reach a climax is proportionately greater than that needed by most men. As a rule, you will get much more pleasure and will be more likely to have an orgasm if your sex sessions last around half an hour or so. However, if your partner only considers his own needs, and lets his pace be governed by his own level of excitement, he will come long before you're anywhere near your climax. In this situation, you're likely to be left feeling frustrated if he thinks lovemaking is over and done with once he's ejaculated. Since it is almost a reflex to many men to fall asleep after climax, it is often better if the female partner's climax is seen to first.

WHAT'S HOLDING YOU BACK?

The good news is that there is almost certainly nothing physically wrong. A few women find that having sexual intercourse or an orgasm causes severe pain or headaches, and this, naturally enough, tends to put them off sex altogether. Anyone who does suffer in this way should go and see her GP. There are a couple of medical treatments that have sometimes been tried in an attempt to solve the problem of being unable to reach a climax:

- Tranquillisers – these drugs are used to soothe anxiety, but as this doesn't seem to be an important factor in women's inability to come, taking them rarely helps with this particular problem.
- Testosterone cream – where has been some research suggesting that using a cream containing this male hormone could make the clitoris more sensitive and so improve the chances of a woman having an orgasm. This isn't often necessary, though, because most women respond to a purely psychological approach to the problem.

There may be many factors in your past or your present life which are contributing to your inability to reach a climax. Do any of the following apply to you?

- You were brought up to believe that sex was 'dirty' and sexual feelings something to be ashamed of.
- You don't like the idea of losing control.

- You're self-conscious about your body or how you look while you're making love.
- You're afraid of looking or sounding foolish.
- An experience in childhood put you off the whole idea of sex.
- You can't relax enough to really enjoy yourself.
- You don't let yourself get too excited because you're afraid you'll be left 'high and dry' after your man has come.

Some people, once they become aware of this kind of hidden agenda, can begin to change with the help of a trusted partner. It may help you simply to be aware that your difficulty with orgasm has its origins in some specific hang-up of this kind – at least if the problem is in your head it is possible to solve it. In fact, sex therapists often aren't especially concerned about why a person has developed this kind of 'block' because the same methods can normally be used to treat it effectively regardless of its origins. In fact, very often there is no specific block at all – it is just a case of the woman's sexual response cycle running at a fairly slow speed and therefore needing plenty of time for climax to happen. The precise approach will vary to some extent depending on the person or the couple concerned, but usually involves suggesting some exercises for them to try at home.

HELP YOURSELF TO AN ORGASM

The first stage for a woman who has never had an orgasm is to discover how to bring herself to a climax through masturbation.

The idea is to make you aware of your own sensations and to discover just what an orgasm actually feels like. You can be as selfish as you like, because you don't have to worry about a partner's feelings or needs, and you can take your time. Like the majority of women, you'll probably find that it helps to fantasise – you can have sex with any man you like in any situation that appeals to you, at least in your imagination. A sexy book or video can help to put you in the mood, and some women find it more pleasurable to stimulate themselves using a vibrator. While orgasm is triggered by sensations in your clitoris, many prefer not to stimulate it directly because it is so sensitive that direct friction can be painful. Stroking and rubbing the surrounding areas of the inner lips is often more pleasurable and arousing, and some women like to have their fingers or something like a candle pushed into their vagina as they come. This is your opportunity to explore your own body and find out what pleases you most sexually, so let yourself really get into it.

You may feel a little uncomfortable about this at first, especially if you come from a family where sex was regarded as something rather shameful and dirty. Touching yourself 'down there' was probably frowned on, to put it mildly, leaving you with the feeling that masturbation was something nice girls simply don't do. As well as learning how to have an orgasm, you also have to overcome this early conditioning. Try to think of your solo sex sessions as a pleasant indulgence, as a treat you're giving yourself, rather than as something furtive. Many women enjoy taking some trouble to set the scene, preparing for it as though they were getting ready for a lovemaking session with a partner. You could begin by taking a warm bath in scented oil, then follow it up by massaging body lotion slowly into your skin, perhaps watching yourself in the mirror as you do it. This gives you the opportunity to find out which parts of your body are most sensitive to touch and stimulation – and you can share your new-found knowledge with your partner later. The most important thing is to take your time, and really enjoy the sensations and the fantasies which excite you. You're aiming to bring out the sensuous creature who is hiding behind your rational exterior. Once the genie is out of the bottle, you won't ever want to put her back inside again!

When you have found out what it feels like to reach a climax and what kind of stimulation is likely to take you there, you can use this new knowledge in sex sessions with your partner. You might like to suggest that he gives you an erotic massage, smoothing oil onto your body as a starter. You can use your experience of your solo sex sessions to guide him to the kind of touch you like best, guiding his hand and giving him signals with words or signs to help him learn what pleases you most. When you are beginning to be aroused, he can move on to stimulating your vulva directly with his hands. Sex therapists often recommend translating the experience of masturbation into shared pleasure in a very direct way. This means asking your partner to put his hand over your genital area, then guiding his movements by putting your own hand on top of his. This means you are taking the lead, and there is less reason to become anxious that your partner will 'take over' and move on to full intercourse before you are ready. Because you are in control, it's easier to relax and concentrate on your physical sensations. An added bonus is that you're teaching your partner how to arouse you and give you the most pleasure. By allowing his hand to be guided by yours, he'll discover where you like to be touched, how much pressure is best and what rhythm pleases you most. You may feel you're being selfish in letting your partner pleasure you in this way without stimulating him in return, but most men find this kind of sexual play very exciting.

His turn can come after you've reached your orgasm, because a woman does not lose all interest in sex once she's climaxed (unlike most men) and you'll probably find you're quite happy to continue making love until your partner is satisfied. The point is that it is not necessary for both partners to be active simultaneously during lovemaking; it is often better to divide the time so that one of you pleasures the other for a considerable period. You can then swap around the active and passive roles when you are ready, or after one of you has had an orgasm, or even next time you make love.

Focus on feeling good

A technique developed by American researchers Masters and Johnson has been widely used to help treat all kinds of sexual difficulties. Known as sensate focus, it is often included as part of a treatment programme under the supervision of a sex therapist, but there's no reason why you shouldn't try it for yourselves at home. The approach is more likely to work when there are no deep-seated or long-standing problems in your relationship with your partner. Although one of the benefits of sensate focus is to improve communication between you as a couple, it may be more successful if you try it after or at the same time as counselling directed towards any specific problems you may have, either as individuals or within your relationship. Remember that any barrier to satisfying sex is much more likely to exist in your psyche than in your body. Once you are in close emotional touch with your partner, your bodies will quickly get the message.

The other name which is sometimes given to the sensate focus technique, 'non-demand pleasuring', sums up what it's all about.

You first have to agree that your sessions won't end in sexual intercourse and, to start with at least, that you won't touch each other's genital areas. The idea is that you take it in turns to caress one another's bodies, touching and stroking to give and receive as much pleasure as you can. One of you starts off being the active toucher, while the other lies back and does nothing at all except to let their partner know when there is something that they especially like or don't like. When you're being the 'toucher', you should try to concentrate as much as you can on your own pleasure in caressing your partner, without worrying unduly about how much pleasure you're giving him or her. With no pressure to progress beyond this caressing stage, you can take all the time you like to explore different parts of your partner's body, and enjoy the feel of their skin and the different contours. In the same way, the person on the receiving end can concentrate exclusively on their own sensations, without the distraction of considering their partner's pleasure. After an agreed amount of time, you swap roles, and the giver becomes the receiver.

When a couple is being treated by a sex therapist, they are usually asked to spend several sessions in this way before moving on to the next stage. Sometimes, one or both partners will find it difficult to relax and give themselves up to erotic sensation, which may mean they need to discuss why this might be happening with their therapist. If, however, you've found this experience enjoyable, you then have further sessions, but now you can touch and explore each other's genitals as well. It's fine if this brings one or both of you to orgasm, although it doesn't matter either if it doesn't, but you are still supposed to avoid intercourse at this stage. In fact, you may find that you want to break the rules, and some couples do this because they become so excited they can't resist it. Although it seems quite simple, sensate focus is very effective as a way of overcoming different kinds of sexual difficulties, in the man as well as the woman. From a woman's point of view, one of its main advantages is that you can relax and enjoy yourself, knowing that the experience won't be cut short because your partner wants to move on to intercourse. Both you and your partner have the opportunity to discover what really turns you on, and you are both 'allowed' to be quite selfish about concentrating on your own erotic and pleasurable sensations.

Many people say that it also improves the communication and trust between them, as you both stick to the prescribed limits and find out things about each other which you didn't know before. From a man's point of view, any concerns he might have about the 'quality' of his performance and whether he is able to satisfy his partner are removed, so he too can relax and enjoy himself.

Where a D-I-Y approach to sensate focus doesn't work, you should think about seeing a therapist. However, when your problems are relatively minor or you just want to make your sex life even more pleasurable, treating yourselves to a period of sensate focus can be exciting and rewarding.

FOR MISSIONARIES ONLY

If you and your partner only ever have intercourse in the so-called 'missionary position', it would not be surprising if the woman finds it difficult or even impossible to have an orgasm through intercourse. With the man lying on top of the woman and between her legs, it is difficult for his penis to provide much stimulation for her clitoris, and she has little control over what is happening. When the man is a bit overweight especially, the woman may even feel unpleasantly smothered in this position.

You are more likely to reach your ultimate goal if you swap positions. Therapists suggest that the couple try letting the woman do all the work and take control. For the male partner, this means lying passively on your back while your partner sits on top of you and guides your penis inside her. You just lie still while she moves up and down on you, experimenting with movements and positions to increase her pleasure. She may like you to stimulate her clitoris at the same time with your hand, or perhaps she will prefer to do this for herself. Just allow yourself to be guided by her – it will be worth it for both of you! For the woman, taking control means treating your partner's penis as a toy and concentrating on your own sensations and what pleases you most. Because your partner isn't moving or thrusting into you, you can take your time and this approach vastly increases your chances of obtaining satisfaction. Meanwhile, you can be sure that he will love watching you. With you on top, he can see and caress or kiss your breasts, and watch your face which will mirror your excitement and pleasure all too clearly. For virtually all men, the certainty that his partner is pleasuring herself with his body and loving the feeling of having him inside her is incredibly exciting, and his orgasm will follow hers within no time at all.

Once a couple has experienced sex which leads to the woman having an orgasm in this way, they often move on to try other positions, such as the man entering from behind, in which he can stimulate his partner's clitoris manually while he is inside her. Once you know it's possible, you can experiment with different positions and different kinds of stimulation to increase your pleasure and find out the best ways to bring the female partner to orgasm. This is best approached in a spirit of trial and error. There are plenty of books around which explain various possible positions in considerable detail, usually with the help of very explicit illustrations. By all means refer to these if you want to but, for many people, 'doing it by the book' can take a lot of the passion and spontaneity out of sex. Apart from anything else, some of the positions involve such incredible acrobatics that they look more like feats of endurance than fun. By experimenting for yourself, you will discover in the nicest possible way what feels good to you. What's more, different approaches will appeal depending on your mood at the time. The so-called 'rear entry' positions, for example, where the man penetrates his partner from behind, are quite animal-like and aggressive and allow the man freedom to thrust as hard as he wants to, while the woman can't move very much. The variations on the 'missionary position', on the other hand, are much more intimate, because you can kiss and watch each other's faces while having intercourse. And of course, there's absolutely no reason why should you confine yourselves to one position – provided the man can control his ejaculation for long enough, you can swap around and enjoy the different sensations offered by making love in different positions for as long as you want. Indeed, withdrawing for a moment and then resuming in a new position is a great way of slowing down a man's climax and teasing a woman to greater heights of arousal. There are no real rules, but the one thing to keep in mind is that much of a woman's sexual pleasure comes from having her clitoris and the surrounding area stimulated. A man who remembers that is likely to have much less trouble in bringing his partner to orgasm.

GETTING IN TOUCH

Do you and your partner ever talk about your sex life, especially about what you like best? If the answer is no, you're probably in the majority. You may well be able to discuss everything from religion to politics, work to health and know everything about each other's favourite foods, holidays and friends without ever discussing the intimate details of your sex life together. Maybe the very thought makes you curl up with embarrassment, or perhaps you feel that your partner should know intuitively what you like to do in bed without you having to spell it out crudely. The fact is, no lover, however sensitive, can read your mind without some clues from you. This doesn't have to mean indulging in anatomical conversations about just where you want him to put his hand and how you like her to hold your penis. In fact, this is more likely to be a turn-off for most people, turning an intimate sharing of pleasure into something that feels more like an obstacle course to be successfully negotiated. The idea is to let one another know what pleases you, and you can do this just as easily with smiles, sighs, touch and by using simple words like 'more, please' or 'that feels good'. Again, compliments are preferable to criticisms and prohibitions as a way of improving your lover's technique.

Women in particular often complain that sex with their partner feels too anonymous: 'He just goes for what he wants and I feel it could be anyone, because he takes no notice of what I'm feeling.' A more common complaint from a man is that his partner seems uninterested or unresponsive; 'She doesn't seem very involved and is never the one to begin sex or make me feel she wants me too.' These may not apply to you and your partner, but the chances are that they do!

The real problem here is often lack of communication. Although both partners would like things to be different, neither knows how to go about changing them. It's hardly surprising then if sex in these circumstances ends up being satisfying for the man in a purely physical sense but nothing more, and pretty uninteresting altogether for the woman. Once you recognise the problem, it's not too difficult to put it right. If you each make an effort to be more aware of your own and your partner's sensations and responses while you're making love, you will soon develop your own 'language' to convey what feels good. It doesn't matter whether you opt for earthy language – some people find this exciting when they try it – or whether you communicate through moans and sighs, or simply use your hands to guide your partner into doing what you enjoy. The aim is to learn how to give and receive more pleasure, and in the process you will both be likely to have more and better orgasms.

How other people feel

Many women feel disinclined to share the more intimate secrets of the bedroom with their friends, although they may have endless conversations about the emotional and practical aspects of relationships. The very idea of getting together with a load of other women to discuss sex and whether you have orgasms may seem quite alien, perhaps even a betrayal of your partner, but in fact it can be very rewarding once you get over the initial shyness. There are women's groups around the country which meet specifically to discuss and share experiences of sexual problems, including the inability to have an orgasm. As well as leading the discussion, the woman running the group may teach the members how to examine themselves, exercise techniques to strengthen the vaginal muscles and improve your control of them and she may also give advice on how to get satisfaction through masturbation.

A related approach is known as 'sexual attitude restructuring', and is designed to break down the barriers which stop so many people talking about sex and how they feel about it. It involves a group of people meeting for a weekend for brainstorming sessions, including sexually explicit films and open discussion. As well as improving communication by taking away the embarrassment, many people find the sessions teach them a lot about sex which they didn't know before. These two aspects – sex education and encouraging open discussion – make this approach very productive for people with all kinds of sexual problems, including orgasm difficulty.

WHEN THE MAN CAN'T COME

If you as a woman find it difficult or even impossible to have an orgasm from intercourse with your partner, you at least have the comfort of knowing that you are far from being alone. A man who experiences the same problem is a relative rarity. It may be that his ejaculation is delayed longer than he or his partner would like – although, for the reasons explained above, this is less likely to be perceived as a problem by the woman. 'The longer the delay the better' may well be her attitude. There are, nevertheless, some men who can't reach a climax at all, however long sex goes on for, and both partners are likely to regard this as a genuine problem. The man is naturally frustrated, while the woman may worry that it is in some way her 'fault' – although this is rarely the case in reality. You will almost certainly need professional help in resolving the difficulty, because the root of the problem needs to be uncovered, and the treatment will depend on the cause.

Of course, the factors affecting you as an individual man will be a unique combination arising from your personal life experience, but therapists have identified some common features which are relevant to many of the men they see:

- Regarding sex almost entirely as a means of fathering a child, rather than as something to be valued for its own sake.
- Conscious or unconscious resistance to the idea of making his partner pregnant and becoming a father. Some men can only ejaculate if they are certain that it can't possibly lead to a pregnancy, perhaps because they have trained themselves in this way and can't later reverse the inhibition. Excessive use of *coitus interruptus* (or the withdrawal method of contraception) can become a habit that is difficult to break out of.
- Feelings of anger against or hostility towards women which the man is unaware of, and which may have grown out of some childhood experience.
- A fear of losing control.
- Feelings of anxiety or guilt, which might be due to some earlier experience or to problems in his relationship with his current partner.
- A physical cause related to something like the use of drugs or alcohol, or to the nerve supply to the penis.
- Increasing age makes a man less likely to be a premature ejaculator, although it's more common to need extra time to become fully erect than it is to suffer from retarded ejaculation.

Whatever is at the root of any one man's problem, it is unlikely that he will be able to sort out his difficulties without professional help. A sympathetic and well-informed GP may be able to offer the necessary treatment or the man may need to be referred to a specialist sex counsellor. Treatment will most often consist of a combination of psychotherapy and the kind of practical 'retraining' used to help men suffering from premature ejaculation (see pages 52–60).

CHAPTER 4

ALL OVER TOO SOON

When a man comes too soon, he is said to be suffering from premature ejaculation, or 'hair trigger trouble'. Before we can consider how this can be overcome, however, we need to work out just what it means.

The man himself may well say, if asked, that there isn't a problem at all. He enjoys sex with his partner, and always has an orgasm which leaves him feeling satisfied. As long as he comes, 'too soon' has little or no meaning for him. At the other extreme, a woman might say that if her partner reaches his climax before she has had time to reach her own, then he is suffering from premature ejaculation. The researchers Masters and Johnson opted for a more moderate definition, calling a man a premature ejaculator if he reached orgasm too soon to satisfy his partner on more than 50 per cent of occasions. This view, which takes no account of how long a woman may take to come, is controversial. Some people would say it is simply another way of describing a woman's inability to reach orgasm.

Research by Kinsey in America suggested that around 75 per cent of men reach orgasm within two minutes of entering their partner's vagina, which will usually be well before the woman is anywhere near coming. It's obvious that, if true, this discrepancy would mean that a man and a woman would be likely to have very different ideas about how soon is too soon.

Some men experience still faster reactions, which everyone would agree are problematic. A man who comes before he has penetrated his partner or even he before he has taken his trousers off can certainly be said to suffer from premature ejaculation by anyone's standards. A few men even ejaculate (or at least produce semen) before they get an erection. Obviously, the age and experience of the man are relevant factors – a teenage boy having sex for the first time in his life with a girl he greatly fancies is unlikely to be able to contain himself for very long, whereas the man who comes too quickly with his wife on their ruby wedding anniversary is more unusual.

WHOSE PROBLEM IS IT ANYWAY?

Despite having all the natural instincts, none of us is born knowing the secrets of successful lovemaking. Our first sexual encounters are likely to be somewhat fumbling, and young men in particular may take time to realise that there's more to it than 'Wham, bam, thank you ma'am.' One aspect of this is learning how to control their high levels of excitement. Sexual intercourse is a novel experience, and may even be a little bit nerve-wracking, so subtlety and consideration for his partner's feelings rarely feature prominently in a man's early encounters. Given more practice, he can develop a greater degree of patience and harness his undoubted enthusiasm with a little more technique. Most young men who experience premature ejaculation in these circumstances will get over it quite quickly and without any help, apart from an allowance of patience and encouragement from their partners.

If you or your partner are a young man with a healthy sexual appetite that is hard to control, you might like to turn it to your advantage by adopting what is sometimes called a 'his and hers' approach. The idea is that you exploit a young man's ability to recover relatively quickly after orgasm. Once the man has satisfied his urgent desire with a 'quickie', you begin making love again after he's rested for a few minutes. If you as the woman were unsatisfied after the first time, you may be quite happy to stimulate your partner with kisses and caresses until he is ready for action again. Using your mouth or hands on your partner's penis is one of the most effective ways to reawaken his desire for sex. It's likely that he will take longer to reach his climax the second time around, giving you more pleasure and more opportunity to come. You may find if you try this approach that your partner can manage another encore within a fairly short time, making it even more likely that you will get satisfaction.

Some couples are surprised to learn that it is possible for the man to have intercourse more than once after as little as 10 minutes' rest. Once you do know that it's possible, however, you can have great fun testing the theory for yourself! A variant on this approach is for the man to reach his first orgasm through masturbation. Like many women, you may find watching your partner bring himself off very arousing, and it's also a good way to discover what kind of stimulation he likes to bring him to orgasm. Of course, you may prefer to take on the task yourself – if so, your man will surely appreciate it. Either way, the aim is the same as before; in other words, to assuage his most urgent desire so that he finds it easier to take things more slowly next time, and give greater consideration to his partner's pleasure and satisfaction.

These approaches to delaying the man's orgasm have the virtue of involving both of you, and may in themselves add to your shared enjoyment of sex. Nevertheless, there are other techniques you can try, although some people feel they are more negative because they involve distracting the man from pleasure or deliberately reducing it so he doesn't come so quickly.

Tricks worth trying:

- Focus your thoughts on something other than your sensations – either a neutral subject or something quite off-putting.
- Concentrate on foreplay in which you stimulate your partner and she doesn't reciprocate.

- Wear a condom to reduce your physical sensitivity.
- Use an anaesthetic cream (sold in sex shops) on your penis to reduce sensation and so prolong your performance.
- Try withdrawing every so often and carry on stimulating your partner until you feel the desire to ejaculate subside a little – then start again, perhaps in a new position.

A PROBLEM SHARED . . .

Waiting for time and experience to come to your rescue will usually work when premature ejaculation hasn't yet become 'programmed' into a man's sexual repertoire. Some men, however, don't grow out of this difficulty, perhaps because they haven't recognised it, or possibly for more complex reasons. These could be the result of anxiety, or related to their past experiences of sex. If your first sexual experiences as a young man were hurried, rather tense affairs where speed was of the essence, you may need to 'unlearn' your ability to come as quickly as possible. You may have developed this habit because you got used to having sex in the back of a car in a relatively public place, for example, or in the family home where you were afraid of being discovered by your parents, or even with a prostitute who encouraged you to get the whole thing over with as fast as possible.

Although it is often possible to overcome this problem completely using what sex therapists call the 'squeeze technique', the major obstacle for many couples is in acknowledging to one another that something is wrong. All too often, both simply suffer this unsatisfactory situation in silence, concealing their worry or frustration from each other out of shyness or not wanting to be hurtful. Sometimes it can reach the point where you, as a woman, find sex so unrewarding that you lose interest altogether, or the man becomes so tense and anxious about his inability to satisfy his partner that he becomes almost unable to perform at all. If you're a man who is not in the habit of analysing your feelings and behaviour, you may be tempted to ignore the problem in the hope that it will go away. You may even dismiss any attempt your partner makes to start talking about the situation, fearing that this could open some Pandora's box of problems that you don't want to get into. While this is a perfectly natural reaction, it's simply going to make things worse in the end. You don't have to feel guilty or that you're to blame; what you do have to do is accept that by acknowledging what is happening, you're beginning a process that will almost certainly lead to a much more rewarding sex life for both you and your partner. The first priority then is to find a way of breaking this stalemate caused by non-communication, and preferably before it has gone on for too long and begun to drive a wedge between the two of you.

Ideally, one of you should try to bring the problem out into the open once you become aware that it is not going to go away by itself. This doesn't have to (and actually shouldn't) involve a great dramatic scene. A man could simply tell his partner, perhaps after they've just made love, how much he loves being inside her and how he wishes could he could stay there longer before coming. If you're a woman who wants to help your man to last longer, you could take a similar line, bearing in mind that your man will probably be ultra-sensitive to any note of criticism or complaint. Either way, the emphasis should be on enhancing your sex life in a way that will give both of you more pleasure and satisfaction. However difficult it seems to be the first to say something, you will be glad afterwards, because you'll have overcome the biggest barrier in the way of solving your problem. Now you have a very good chance of getting over your difficulties on your own, using the technique described below. Postponing dealing with the problem, on the other hand, can mean that communication between you as a couple breaks down so far that you need outside help to bring you close enough to use self-help techniques. Sex therapists and GPs who are experienced in treating couples with this kind of sexual difficulty often find they have to help the two people concerned to break down barriers that have been built up between them before they can uncover the real problem and start to tackle it.

LEARNING 'THE SQUEEZE'

The idea behind this technique is that a man is taught to become increasingly aware of the sensations that mean he is approaching orgasm and ultimately to use this awareness to hold back from his climax. Initially, you steer clear of actual penetration altogether, as the woman concentrates on stimulating her partner's penis as he lies on his back and she sits facing him, with his legs straddling hers. She can stroke and rub him or stimulate him with her mouth and tongue to increase his arousal and excitement. At the point when he signals that he is getting near to the point of inevitability, she stops stimulating him and gently squeezes the end of his penis. The way to do this correctly is to hold his penis between your fingers and thumb, just below where the head joins the shaft, then squeeze, especially on the underside. This will stop the man from ejaculating and may cause him to lose his erection, partially, for a while. After a few minutes' rest, you start stimulating him again and go through the same stages as before. You do this several times in one session, before finally you carry on stimulating him until he ejaculates. Either or both of you may find it hard to control your excitement, but the longer you go on and delay orgasm, the better. Some therapists recommend that the man himself takes responsibility for the squeezing as he is more closely in touch with his own sensations. Others believe that the technique will work if you just start and stop stimulation at the right moment, leaving out the actual squeezing bit.

It has to be said that the whole process can seem somewhat clinical and unromantic from the woman's point of view, so you need to keep your sense of humour, and also to remind yourself that it should be worth it in the end. Nevertheless, many women find they really enjoy pleasuring their man in this way and knowing that they have the power to make him come or hold him back as they choose. When a couple is being treated by a sex therapist, they are usually encouraged to move on to having sexual intercourse once the man has achieved a greater awareness and control of his orgasm. They make love with the woman on top, and once again, she withdraws from his penis at the moment when he signals that he is approaching his climax. She then squeezes his penis as before, giving him a few minutes to recover before moving on top of him again and continuing intercourse. In this way, he is able to develop the same awareness of approaching climax as he had when his partner was masturbating him. Eventually, sex is allowed to take its natural course, and though there are bound to be a few occasions when premature ejaculation still occurs, a few weeks of using this technique is all it takes for many couples to begin a more satisfying sex life. By then, the woman will have learned a lot about masturbating her partner which she can put to good use in future lovemaking sessions. What's more, if she hadn't tried it before, she'll have discovered the potential advantages to her of being 'on top', which is one of the best positions for a woman to reach orgasm during intercourse.

'DON'T BLAME ME!'

One of the reasons why couples fail to bring the problem of premature ejaculation into the open is that one or both of them feels guilty or insecure about it. It's all too easy to let yourself think that your sex life is unsatisfactory because you're doing something 'wrong' or because your partner doesn't find you sufficiently attractive. In fact, the opposite is often true – the man becomes highly aroused so quickly by his partner that he can't hold himself back from orgasm. Although many men grow out of this difficulty in time, those who don't usually experience it with any and every woman they make love to – it's not the result of his current partner doing something wrong, so to speak.

It is actually rare for the problem to start suddenly in later life, but it can occasionally begin with a new partner. When this does happen, it may have something to do with the reactions of the woman concerned, or reflect an unresolved problem in their relationship. It has been suggested that some women do everything they can to make their partner come quickly – a technique also used frequently by prostitutes. It could be that this is her way of getting back at the man and humiliating him because of some resentment or unexpressed anger.

Alternatively, it could be that she wants to get sex over with quickly before she can become too aroused because she knows that otherwise she'll end up frustrated. When premature ejaculation is occurring in a situation like this, the squeeze technique is probably not going to appeal, because the fundamental problem in the relationship itself needs to be sorted out first. You may be able to manage this on your own if communication hasn't broken down between you, but couples often find they make more progress when they are able to discuss their difficulties with a neutral outsider, such as a Relate counsellor.

CHAPTER 5

ERECTION PROBLEMS?

A man is said to be suffering from impotence when he can't get an erection or can't stay hard long enough to have intercourse. Some people confuse it with infertility, which means that the man has difficulty in fathering a child, often because of a sperm deficiency. It is important to understand the difference – you could quite well be a 'five times a night' man yet still have fertility problems.

Unlike a woman, a man has no disguises at his disposal. She can pretend to want sex and go through the motions, even pretending to have an orgasm to please her partner, while she is really completely detached and unaroused. While this is hardly to be recommended, it means that she is less likely to feel a failure or that she is letting her partner down because she 'can't' perform. Few women see one or two episodes of this kind as a major drama in their sex lives, whereas a man who can't make love because he can't 'get it up' on a couple of occasions may feel he is under terrific pressure to perform next time. The idea that a 'real man' is ready and eager to have sex at any time is very widespread, so if that doesn't apply to you, you can end up feeling ashamed and embarrassed. The truth is that very many men experience this problem at some time in their lives, often for several years, without seeking or receiving help.

Men who do seek help mostly expect to be told by their doctor that there is something physically wrong with them – an undiagnosed illness or a hormone imbalance – to account for their impotence. This possibility will need to be investigated, because there are some conditions (as well as some medical treatments) which result in impotence, but even when this is the case, there are frequently psychological factors involved as well. Very often, there is nothing amiss physically, and the cause of the difficulties must be sought in the man's personality and/or in his relationship with his partner.

A PHYSICAL EXPLANATION?

Your doctor's first task is to make absolutely sure that there is no physical problem. He or she will want to examine you, and will also ask about your medical history. He or she will probably want to know:

- Do you ever wake up with an erection in the morning? When your answer is yes, it implies that there's nothing wrong with your 'plumbing' and the cause must be looked for elsewhere.
- Do you regularly drink large quantities of alcohol? The trouble here is that while drinking makes you lose your inhibitions so you're more likely to want sex, it also makes it more difficult to get and keep an erection – the infamous 'brewer's droop', well-known to regular drinkers.
- Do you have diabetes? Even when the answer is apparently no, your blood or urine may be tested to make sure, as many people in middle to later life develop so-called type II (or non insulin-dependent) diabetes without being aware of it. One possible complication of this condition is damage to the blood circulation and the nerves which can interfere with erections.
- What prescription medicines if any are you taking? It is being increasingly recognised that some drugs – such as beta-blockers used to treat high blood pressure – may cause potency problems as a side effect.
- Do you have any other health problems, such as heart

or circulatory disease, or other unexplained symptoms? Your GP will want to check you out as there are certain conditions which will need to be excluded as the cause. Candidates include multiple sclerosis, tumours and hormonal disturbances, although it must be stressed that it is much more likely that the cause will be found to be psychological rather than physical.

- Do you feel that your life is particularly stressful, or that everyday problems are getting on top of you? Anxiety and depression often mean the sufferer loses interest in many of the activities he used to enjoy, including sex, and it's hardly surprising if he has potency problems.

Even if your answers to the questions above are all negative, your doctor may well want to arrange for a few tests just in case there is some physical problem which is not immediately apparent. You will probably have samples of blood taken, so these can be analysed at the laboratory to check the levels of various hormones. The results of these may indicate some specific problem which needs further investigation and treatment.
In some circumstances, this is fairly straightforward – the condition is successfully treated or existing treatment changed or modified, and the impotence disappears along with the cause. Where this is not practical – because the blood supply to the penis is not working properly, for example – more direct intervention may be needed. This could perhaps mean surgery to the penis to improve its blood supply, injections which produce a temporary, 'artificial', erection or an implant which makes the penis permanently firm but pliable. These are rather extreme measures, however, and only necessary in a minority of cases. Alternative 'mechanical' aids to erection have been developed, such as suction pumps and mechanical restriction rings which you

fit round the base of the penis. Some even have metal plates that are supposed to produce an electrical current when in contact with the skin (the 'Blakoe Ring'). You may see them in sex shops or advertised for sale by mail order, but you should get medical advice before using any of them. Some are useless and they may even be dangerous. It's also worth mentioning that the solution many men expect to be offered – injections or tablets containing the male hormone testosterone – are more likely to be tried only as a last resort. There are some private clinics offering this treatment as a kind of hormone replacement therapy for men. Testosterone may be beneficial if the doctors have reason to believe that a man's own natural supply of the hormone is deficient for some reason, but opponents of this approach argue that the side effects are not well understood. What's more, they suggest that any benefit is likely to be short-lived because the body will compensate for the effects of the treatment by reducing its own output of testosterone still further.

IT'S YOUR AGE!

If you're a woman of 'a certain age' – in other words, anything over 40 – you will almost certainly have got used to the fact that any minor physical or psychological problem is put down to your time of life. 'You have to expect it at your age' is the common response, even when age plainly has nothing to do with the matter in hand. Men, however, don't have this great hurdle of the menopause looming ahead of them, and so are inclined to expect that they will continue just as fit and functioning as they've always been, regardless of the passage of time. This probably explains why so many men first go to see their doctors complaining of potency problems at around the age of 50.

When you start to notice that you're not getting erections as often as you once did, or that they're less hard or long lasting, you may well wonder whether you're suffering from some mysterious illness. It's much more likely, though, that all you're really suffering is the physical changes which occur naturally with age. So, the first message is 'Don't panic!' This is not the beginning of the end as far as your sex life is concerned, but rather the start of a new and potentially interesting phase. Even though seeing your partner in the nude may no longer be enough to give you an erection straight away, especially if you've been together for some time, some extra stimulation will usually do the trick.

It has to be said too that boredom with a long-time sexual partner can contribute to a man's potency problems more often than people like to admit. When the two of you have been together for a long time, it's all too easy to allow your sex life to become routine and more of a habit than a pleasure. Some experts believe that men are biologically programmed to look for variety in their sexual partners, and so may need to make more of an effort than women to nurture feelings of desire for their familiar partners. Even if you doubt that this could be a factor in your own erectile problems, you've nothing to lose and could have a lot to gain by encouraging her to join you in a little sexual experimentation.

It's not always easy to bring up the subject when you and your partner have always been used to what might be called straightforward sex, but it's worth the effort. It might help if you and your partner go through the short questionnaire overleaf, answering the questions separately and then comparing notes. The idea is to consider the various kinds of erotic stimulation available, and find some that appeal to you both.

Would you like your partner to give you a sensual massage?

When you don't feel ready to make love, being given a full body massage by your partner is an enjoyable alternative. With a low light and peaceful surroundings, you can simply lose yourself in the physical sensations, perhaps using suitable music to create the mood. Some people prefer to keep conversation to a minimum too, so you could try and signal to your partner or say the odd word to indicate when you would like him or her to concentrate on a particular area, press harder or more lightly or whatever. Depending on your mood, a massage can be a purely relaxing experience or one full of sensual pleasure which ends with you both feeling so aroused you find you do want to make love after all.

Would you like to be the one giving the massage?

This is one of the nicest ways to relax and share close intimacy with your partner. Not only does it ease the tension caused by the stresses and strains of everyday life, but it can also help to relieve pain from stiff muscles and joints or minor injuries. You'll need to use oil – vegetable-based ones are best – and you can buy lightly scented ones ready mixed from such places as The Body Shop. Remember that if you use essential oils, they need to be well diluted with a 'carrier' oil. A woman who is pregnant or thinks she might be should be extra careful to avoid using undiluted oils, and some varieties should be avoided altogether. Look for labels on the bottles or leaflets or ask an assistant if in doubt.

The bed may be a bit too soft, but a hard surface, such as a thigh-high table or the floor is ideal. Make sure the room is warm, and pour the oil on to your hands to warm it first rather than directly on to your partner's skin. You don't need to be a trained masseur to do this, just keep your movements rhythmic and circular, and explore the shape and feel of your partner's body. Generally speaking, stroking the muscles firmly up the body (against the sagging caused by gravity) is particularly satisfying, with lighter pressure on the downward strokes. And it is usually most exciting if the genitals are saved until last.

There aren't really any rules – you can vary the degree of pressure from very firm to feather light – just do what feels right to both of you.

Would you enjoy taking a bath or a shower with your partner, soaping each other all over?

This is another simple but fun way to enjoy physical closeness with your partner and begin to break away from the ordinary bedroom routine. Like massage, it's a novel way for the two of you to explore one another's bodies and enjoy the feel of slippery skin and close contact without feeling any pressure to go further unless you want to. In fact, many people tell researchers that they enjoy making love in the bathroom, and there's no reason why you shouldn't try this too if bathing or showering together excites you. Otherwise, just use soap or shower gel, exploring every part of your partner's body before turning your attention to their genitals. Don't push soap inside the vagina though, as this will interfere with the natural lubrication and may even cause thrush. Whether you get into the bath or shower together or one of you stays outside is up to you. And if you don't want to make love afterwards, dry one another gently in big soft towels with lots of cuddles.

Would you like to watch a sexy film with your partner?

You may need to do a bit of advance planning if you have never done this before – some couples automatically switch over or off when they know a sexually explicit film is about to start on TV. If you have a video, you could choose one that appeals, otherwise you'll have to check the TV schedules to see what's coming on that you would like to see. Perhaps you could persuade your partner by suggesting that you watch something which has caused a certain amount of comment or controversy: 'Everybody's been talking about this one – isn't it about time we found out what all the fuss is about?' A bottle of wine or a couple of gin and tonics will relax you and help overcome any potential embarrassment.

Would you like to read sexy books or magazines in bed together?

If you've never done this before, you could start with something fairly 'soft' – many women's magazines and ordinary novels include quite frank sexual material these days. Try to pick something which you think will interest your partner, then try reading a bit out loud or hand it over for him or her to read – 'This bit is amazing; you must read it.' Remember that while a man is more likely to be turned on by photos of naked women, a woman will probably prefer an article or story which includes some plotting and characterisation or the story of real people.

Would you like to try some of the popular sex toys, such as a vibrator or dildo (artificial penis)?

Whether you start by discussing the possibility in theory or actually buy something as a surprise depends on you and your relationship. Some people who would be horrified at the idea of trying any sex toys find they enjoy using them once they've tried and discovered what fun can be had. On the other hand, if you feel your partner would prefer to be involved in deciding what to try and choosing together, you could either look at advertisements in the back of a sex magazine or get hold of a catalogue from one of the companies who advertise there and elsewhere.

Would you like to try something you have never done before (such as oral sex, perhaps) or have intercourse in unusual places or positions?

Sexy films, videos or magazines are probably the easiest way to introduce this idea – then you can simply say at the appropriate moment – 'I wonder what that would be like' or 'I've always fancied trying that – what do you think?' If your sex life has always been rather unadventurous until now, you might like to get hold of one of the recent sex education videos or the large illustrated sex encyclopaedias as these will actually show you some suggestions to stimulate your imagination.

Is there something special you would like your partner to do for you sexually? If so, what?

The secret here, as with so much to do with good sex, is communication. There's no way your partner can know what you want unless you tell him or her. At the very least, give some sign by guiding what he or she does during lovemaking. Again, you can use videos or magazines as a starting point and see how your partner reacts to what you would like. Perhaps he or she will be enthusiastic or at least willing, but you do have to be prepared for the opposite response. Perhaps a little gentle persuasion of a reluctant partner may be all right, but anything more is not acceptable – 'No' has to mean what it says.

Is there something you would like to do for him/her? If so, what?

The same applies here as in the previous point – communication is the key. Depending on just what you have in mind, you may be able to make a move in the right direction to test your partner's response. Otherwise the answer is to come out with it – 'I'd really love to bring you off with my mouth' or whatever it may be – and see whether the suggestion is welcome.

Do you have a favourite sexual fantasy that you could share with your partner?

The best time to share a fantasy with your partner is when you are both already aroused and beginning to make love. Even then, you shouldn't just carry on regardless – take it slowly while you try to sense how your partner is responding to what you're saying. Most people don't react well to the idea that their partner has a fantasy about a real person known to them, for fear that they will one day put it into practice. Only go into more detail if and when you get the feeling that your partner is responsive and sympathetic. The same goes for memories of wild carnal experiences from your past that involved someone other than your present partner; some people find that swapping such stories is titillating, but jealousy and anger are more common reactions.

As you can see, there are so many ways for a loving couple to spice up their sex life that you should be able to find some that you'd both like to explore. Once you accept that you need a little more stimulus than you used to and start experimenting, the results will almost certainly compensate for the effects of aging.

LOOK AFTER YOURSELF

Unless we are ill, most of us take our bodies for granted, and don't give much thought to keeping them in good condition until they let us down. Men in particular often pay far less attention to maintaining their health than they do to maintaining their cars. It's only when something starts to go wrong that they begin to take notice, and look for a quick fix from the doctor instead of thinking about what might have caused the problem. A recent report showed that only around 10 per cent of men in this country follow a regular fitness programme, and being overweight and indulging in a dodgy diet are all too common. Read through our quick fitness checklist to see where you fall down:

- Have you put on more than a pound or two in weight over the last 10 years?
- Do you eat junk food such as burgers and chips or chocolate bars more than once or twice a week?
- Do you make sure you include several portions of fresh fruit, vegetables and salad in your diet every day?
- Do you smoke?
- Do you spend several hours a day behind the wheel of a car, or often travel by plane or train?
- Do you work long hours or often have to work away from home?

- Do you take any kind of regular exercise – the sort that doesn't just involve raising your right arm?
- Do you regularly drink more than 21 units of alcohol a week? (One unit means a small glass of wine, a single measure of spirits or half a pint of beer.)
- Can you remember when you last had a medical check-up?

While it may be impossible to avoid stress, you'll cope with it far better if you give your body a good chance of fighting back. Stopping smoking, eating a balanced diet and taking regular exercise are guaranteed ways to boost your overall health and fitness. Keeping your cardiovascular system in trim is undoubtedly good for your libido and helps fight off depression. Obesity and ill health will do your sexual prowess no favours at all. However, you should beware of diets that focus on restriction (either of calories or cholesterol). It is important to eat well and make sure you're properly nourished. Although an excessively high level of cholesterol is bad for your heart, the brain needs a certain amount of cholesterol to function properly. It is the building block of sex hormones and neurotransmitters. Therefore, it is better to eat good food than to starve yourself, and exercising is a much healthier way to lose weight.

When you don't know why . . .

Sometimes it is simple to establish that there is no physical reason why a man can't have a normal erection, and it's not just his age either. In these circumstances, the explanation must lie somewhere in his psyche and/or in his relationship. As with all sexual problems, it's unrealistic to expect to resolve the sexual difficulty when the real problem is rooted in the way the two individuals involved relate to one another. This is sometimes made very obvious to sex therapists when a man whose wife says he is impotent privately confesses to stud-like prowess with other women. Helping a couple in this situation is difficult, especially when the woman concerned is not let in on the secret.

Where the relationship has gone wrong, you may need outside help to sort it out, and there's probably no point in trying to deal with your sexual difficulties until you've worked the problems through. Once this has been done, or if you feel that you are already close enough to be able to tackle the erection difficulties together, you can take the first steps towards repairing your love life. It may sound obvious, but you can't get anywhere until you acknowledge openly that there is a problem – and that it's one that you share.

NOT JUST HIS PROBLEM

A woman whose man has erection problems may go through as much emotional pain and frustration as he does, unless the situation can be discussed openly. If you are the partner of such a man, you are going to feel not only frustrated, but probably also angry, guilty, confused and lacking in confidence at various times. Eventually, you may switch off altogether and lose interest in sex, or alternatively be tempted to look elsewhere.

A man who is angry and confused about his inability to have an erection may lash out at his partner and blame her. Sex therapists often hear men in this position say that they wouldn't have the problem if their partner were more attractive/thinner/

less of a nag or whatever. Some will even say that they can't make love to a woman who is assertive and confident and that it's all the fault of the feminist movement. It is vital to sort out whether this is just the way an angry man tries to shift the 'blame' for his sexual failure, or whether it indicates that there is a real problem in the couple's relationship which needs sorting out. It's also worth pointing out that impotence existed long before anyone ever thought about feminism. In any case, arguing about whose fault it is is pointless and will only make the problem worse. Certainly, it is counter-productive for a woman to humiliate her partner for his sexual failure.

It is important to try and break out of this destructive mind-set by facing the problem together if it is at all possible. As a woman, you need to be reassured that your partner still loves you and thinks you desirable, even if he is unable to prove it for the time being. He needs to know the same, and if your relationship is good enough for you to be able to help one another, you have a sound basis on which to start rebuilding your sex life. You will need to be prepared to be especially loving and patient, and recognise that it will take time to restore your man's sexual self-confidence. It helps if you can put your own feelings of resentment or deprivation to one side, and keep reminding yourself that you will have a lot to gain in the long term by making a fresh start now.

LEARNING TO MAKE LOVE AGAIN

Impotence sometimes follows on from a couple of occasions when the man's erection has failed him, so that he becomes worried that the same thing will happen every time he tries to have sex. Mind and body are so closely linked that his anxiety stops him from relaxing and letting nature take its course, and so his worries become a self-fulfilling prophecy. In a way, the problem is worse now than for previous generations of men because they are aware that making love should be pleasurable for both partners. At one time, a man didn't need to give any thought to how well he was performing – in other words, whether he was giving his partner satisfaction as well as himself. Now that there is, quite rightly, more notice taken of whether a woman is enjoying sex, and more coverage in the media generally about male sexual technique, there is much more pressure on a man. If he feels that he is inadequate as compared to other men, this helps to set up a vicious circle of anxiety and fear of failure. Finding himself impotent on the odd occasion is more difficult to dismiss, and the worry almost guarantees that it will happen again next time he tries to have sex.

You may both find it quite a relief to put a ban on all attempts at intercourse while you work on the problem together. Once you both accept that a lovemaking session is definitely not intended to lead to penetration, you can relax and enjoy yourselves. The technique known as sensate focus or non-demand pleasuring (see pages 40 to 42) can be a delightful way to enjoy the pleasure of sensual foreplay and rediscover sensations you'd forgotten (or never knew) you could feel. When treatment is under the guidance of a sex therapist, the ban on sexual intercourse usually stays until it becomes clear that the couple is ready to move on. In practice, however, no one is likely to reproach a couple who get carried away by passion and have sex before they're supposed to. Nevertheless, it is better to go extra slowly than to try and rush things and attempt to have intercourse before both of you are truly ready. If in doubt, leave it a little longer. For a man who fears (or knows) that he has been disappointing his partner sexually, it is often enlightening to find out how much foreplay she can enjoy without becoming impatient or frustrated. He may well also discover that she has more and better orgasms while intercourse is banned than she ever had when it wasn't!

A CAUTIONARY NOTE

Sadly, and regardless of what you may have heard or read elsewhere about the miraculous properties of rhino horn, oysters or any other exotic substances, there is no such thing as a conveniently available and effective aphrodisiac. Most simply don't work at all, and some, such as amyl nitrite (poppers) and Spanish Fly can be positively dangerous. Spanish Fly is actually a drug called cantharidin, and if you swallow it, it can irritate your stomach, kidneys and urethra and can actually be fatal. It is made from dried southern European beetles, and if that's not enough to put you off, a legend reported by two American academics may do the trick. The powder was apparently used in sixteenth century Provence as a cure for fever. One woman reported that after taking it, her husband made love to her 40 times within 48 hours, then dropped dead!

There are several promising substances currently being investigated for their aphrodisiac properties, although a great deal more research is still needed into their effectiveness and, of course, their side effects.

- Yohimbine – an alkaloid derived from the bark of a West African tree.
- Ginseng – from the root of a Chinese plant.

- Vitamin E – contained naturally in wheatgerm.
- L-dopa and other chemicals which boost or mimic dopamine, a substance found naturally in the brain. One such chemical has been somewhat unromantically dubbed LY163502 by the scientists studying it.

Unfortunately, none of these substances has so far shown any consistent, uncontroversial effect.

Chemists have made various attempts to imitate substances called pheromones produced by the human body which seem to play a role in attracting and exciting the opposite sex. Most commonly, these are emitted by males in order to 'turn on' females and so have little relevance to potency problems. Some sex shops sell a spray-on aphrodisiac made from the pheromone androstenol, found in the sweat and urine of male pigs. Unfortunately, many women say it smells as horrible as it sounds, although it seems to work all right on female pigs. Musk, which is an ingredient of many perfumes, comes from the scent glands of male deer, and is supposed to excite humans too. This may contain an element of truth, but many men and women actually prefer the natural smell of their partner to an overpowering cloud of perfume, however exotic and expensive.

CHAPTER 6

VAGINAL TIGHTENING

If you are a woman with vaginismus (vaginal tightening), you have probably never been able to have full sexual intercourse at all, or you may have managed it but found it painful. It's also likely that you've never been able to use tampons. Like a lot of women with this problem, you are most likely to think that it's a matter of size – in other words, your vagina is too small or tight to let either a tampon or an erect penis inside. You may well have assumed that this is because your body is in some way abnormal, or that it has simply been made too small. The truth is that such abnormalities are extremely rare, and are almost certainly not the reason why you are unable to accept anything inside your vagina.

WHAT IS VAGINISMUS?

What actually happens is that when you are faced with the immediate prospect of penetration, the muscles around the entrance to your vagina tighten up. This can make it impossible for your partner's penis to enter, or painful for you if he does manage it. The fact that you are in pain naturally means you don't enjoy the experience, and would prefer to avoid it as far as possible. Because sexual intercourse is difficult if not completely impossible, making love can end up being a pretty tense and miserable experience, and very distressing for both of you. It is all too easy for either or both of you to blame yourselves or each other, but this isn't justified either. You don't tighten your muscles deliberately or even consciously, and although the problem is sometimes blamed on a partner's roughness or clumsiness, this isn't often relevant in reality. Many women with vaginismus have partners who are gentle and compliant types. They often accept the situation without much of a fuss, which is one reason why the women may not have the incentive to ask for professional help. Some men even seem to adapt to the fact that they can't have intercourse with their partners by becoming completely or partially impotent themselves.

The severity of the problem varies from one woman to another, but it is quite common, affecting around 20 per cent of the women who attend sex problem clinics and unknown numbers besides. The good news is that very many of these women are eventually able to enjoy a normal sex life after treatment. Knowing this can be the incentive you need to try and solve your problem. Unfortunately, it is very unlikely to go away by itself, so the sooner you can summon up courage to get help, the sooner you and your partner can start looking forward to a better love life.

EXPLORE YOUR OWN BODY

Although, as we've said, it is very unlikely that there's anything physically wrong with you, your GP will probably want to check you out by performing an internal examination, just to make quite sure. For example, any condition which made the outer part of your vagina or your vulva painful could well account for the reflex contraction of the muscles at your vaginal opening. For someone who suffers from vaginismus, the prospect of being examined can be enough to put you off ever going near a doctor's surgery to discuss the problem. However, an experienced doctor will be aware of this, and even if you don't say anything, will be able to tell from your reaction that you are frightened. You might find it less alarming to see a woman doctor if you can, but if you don't feel comfortable about going to the GP's surgery at all, you could make an appointment at the nearest family planning clinic instead. The doctors there will have had plenty of practice examining nervous or even frightened women, and you can be sure of a sympathetic and understanding response.

Often, the doctor will use a special technique to examine someone who is very nervous: after he or she has placed an examining finger at the entrance to your vagina, you will be asked to use your own hand to manoeuvre it inside. The idea is to put you rather than the doctor in control, and it is usually amazingly effective. Many women are astonished to find how easy and painless it is to be examined in this way, and are able to become more relaxed about the whole business. For many, it is the first time they start to believe that they are physically normal and not misshapen in some way, and this can be confirmed by examining themselves. Your doctor may well suggest that you try examining yourself at home so you can learn more about your vagina, and get accustomed to the idea that you can put your fingers inside without pain or difficulty. Sometimes, when a couple has been unable to have intercourse because of vaginismus, the doctor will suggest that your partner comes with you to the surgery to see for himself that everything is normal. If both of you are happy about the idea, your partner can try inserting a finger into your vagina himself. The idea is to convince both of you that you can be penetrated painlessly – it can take a while for this vital fact to sink in when both of you have always assumed it was impossible because of some undiagnosed physical oddity.

Your doctor may well recommend that you practise examining yourself at home – just to get you used to how your body is made and how it feels inside. A good time to try this technique is when you're as relaxed as possible, in the bath, perhaps, or in bed. Practise putting the tip of your finger into your vagina, and keep it there while you consciously tighten and relax your vaginal muscles around it. After a while, you may be able to put one finger inside, and move it around to explore your sensations. It is more fun if you make it part of a solo sex session, combining it with masturbation and imagining yourself into a fantasy situation which excites you. Some women with vaginismus have come to believe that they can't enjoy sex at all or that they don't have the normal responses, but this isn't often true. Nevertheless, you may need to work at destroying the psychological barriers you've built up over the years to avoid becoming aroused because of what it will lead to. Masturbation is a good way to do this, as you begin to discover what pleases you most and to realise how much enjoyment you really can get from sex. Once you become excited, your vagina will produce a natural lubrication which makes it easier for you to slip one or more fingers inside, once the muscles are relaxed. Nevertheless, it may help to begin with some kind of lubricating agent such as skin lotion, Vaseline or KY Jelly.

NOW TWO CAN PLAY

Once you have gained confidence, the next stage is to encourage your partner to learn about your body in the same way. To start with, this could mean you guiding his finger inside you, then allowing him to do this alone. It doesn't sound very sexy, and either or both of you may not like the prospect very much. Nevertheless, if you do manage to try it successfully, it will help both of you to understand that painless penetration is possible despite past problems. After the first few times, once you know it's all right, you may start to enjoy it and can turn it into part of your love play with your partner. It helps if you try not to be too 'clinical' about it. Keep your explorations until you are both in a sexy mood, and treat the exercise as a part of lovemaking, caressing and talking to each other, bringing in any fantasies that you both find arousing. At first, you may not produce any natural lubrication, so again, it is a good idea to have massage oil or a vaginal lubricant such as KY Jelly or Senselle available to make things more comfortable.

Many couples get on so well with this kind of therapeutic sex play that they gain the confidence to go further. Many men enjoy being made love to by their partner while they remain relatively passive, and for a woman who is learning to enjoy intercourse this is a good approach too. You'll probably still feel a bit nervous about the prospect of your partner putting his erect penis inside you even though you now know that you are big enough to take it. It will help you to relax if you and your partner agree that you will be the one who controls what happens and when. That way, you can go as slowly as you like, secure in the knowledge that your partner won't try to enter you unless or until you are ready for him. Postponing the crucial moment for as long as possible is something that many women would like to do anyway given the chance because, as we saw in chapter 1, a woman usually takes longer to become fully aroused than a man.

Once you feel confident that penetration is possible and potentially enjoyable, get your man to lie on his back while you lower yourself gently on to his erection. The idea is for him to remain completely passive and still so you can feel totally in control of what is happening. That way, you'll have much less reason to panic, and it's up to you to decide when you feel ready to explore the sensations of moving and thrusting.

This kind of step-by-step approach is probably best carried out under the guidance of your doctor or a sex therapist, but there's no reason why you shouldn't try it for yourselves at home if you want to. When you have been living with the problem of vaginismus for months or even years, anything which might help you to relax and get over it is worth a try. Many women – and their partners – find to their surprise that what starts as a way of overcoming fear turns before long into an activity that they enjoy for its own sake.

Sorting your head out

As we've said, it is rare for there to be any physical problem that is stopping you from having sexual intercourse – the barrier is usually more a psychological or emotional one, possibly connected to something in your past. When talking to a woman who is suffering from vaginismus, the therapist often discovers that the client enjoys masturbation and has normal sexual responses in other respects. Alternatively, her inability to enjoy sexual intercourse may have led her to 'shut down' her sexual responses altogether, so she believes that she is just one of those people with a very low sex drive. Either way, there is normally some reason why a barrier has been built up which makes penetration of her vagina unacceptable. Some women can be helped to find a way past this barrier without needing to focus on the reason for its existence, as we saw above. Whether your past needs to be unravelled to reveal what is behind your sexual difficulty depends a lot on your own personal situation. Even when the root of the problem lies in something like sexual abuse in childhood, a repressive attitude to sex instilled by your parents or the fact that your first attempts to have sex were painful, it's not always necessary to explore the experience in depth. It may be possible to overcome your sexual difficulty in the 'here and now', although some women will still need counselling to help them deal with the psychological and emotional complexities of their past. Your GP should be able to refer you to the right source of help – it may be a clinical psychologist, for example, a psychotherapist or a counsellor who specialises in helping the victims of past sexual abuse. Naturally, exploring such problems isn't easy – and can be painful as well as very hard work – but if you are able to come to terms with your past, your future will look a lot brighter.

GOING IT ALONE

Of course, you may be one of those women who feel that your difficulty is not severe enough to need professional help, whether from your GP, a sex therapist or a psychotherapist. You may experience vaginismus because lovemaking has not so far allowed for the fact that you, like nearly all women, take much longer to become sexually aroused and ready for intercourse than a man does. When you are not sufficiently excited, you won't produce any natural lubrication and it's very likely that it will hurt when your partner tries to put his penis inside you. The pain may well cause your muscles to go into spasm. If this has happened to you a few times, it's hardly surprising if your body says 'No thanks' to any repeat performances. What's probably going wrong here is that familiar factor – impatience. Unless your partner is willing to spend a reasonable amount of time stimulating you so that you get excited and your body prepares itself for sex, you aren't likely to get much – if any – pleasure. Your man is certainly not alone in not realising this – probably no one has ever taken the trouble to explain to him that time and patience are qualities no skilled lover should be without. Someone has to tell him, so why not you? After all, you both have a lot to gain in terms of a happier and more rewarding love life. Obviously, this doesn't mean sitting him down and making him listen to a lecture on female sexual response! It's not a good idea either to make your explanation sound critical; 'You always go at it so fast that it's all over before

I've started to warm up' is unlikely to achieve your desired aim. Far better to begin his education when you are feeling close and intimate, perhaps when you are beginning to make love. Choose a time when you know there'll be nothing to disturb you for a while, and encourage him to caress and stimulate you – if you enjoy having your breasts kissed, for example, you could ask him to keep on doing it, saying how much you like it. Be positive and tell him that you enjoy making love with him so much you want it to last as long as possible. To start with, his idea of a long time may still be less than yours, but once he sees the effect on you of foreplay, he'll begin to appreciate the benefits. Once he's beginning to get the idea, he might be encouraged to sample the delights of non-penetrative sex, by trying the technique of sensate focus (non-demand pleasuring). For a woman who avoids arousal because lovemaking never lasts long enough for her to reach orgasm, this is a good way to discover (or rediscover) the sensations her body is capable of experiencing. To find out more about this technique, turn to page 40 and read it with your partner. The form of sex therapy known as sensate focus is really just a kind of loveplay, although it was originally developed by the American therapists Masters and Johnson to help couples with all kinds of sexual difficulties. One of its main advantages is that it takes away the 'pressure to perform', so that you learn to experience and enjoy being touched and caressed without worrying whether your vaginal muscles will cooperate when it comes to penetration.

From a Man's Point of View

You were probably surprised and upset – as well as frustrated – when you first realised that your partner was unable to enjoy sexual intercourse with you. You may even have felt angry – 'Why hadn't she said something before?' – or worried that you were somehow responsible for the debacle. However, you have to realise that it's a very brave woman who is able to reveal this problem to a new partner before they first make love, in case it frightens him off altogether. She perhaps hoped or imagined that the problem was specific to her relationship with her previous partner and would not arise with the new one. And once the initial shock is over, you still have to come to terms with the probability that this problem isn't going to go away by itself, however much you love each other. Although both of you will find the situation difficult at times, there are good reasons why you shouldn't give up on the idea of eventually being able to make love to your partner.

- There is every reason to hope that in time your partner will be able to overcome her problem – with your help.
- In the meantime, you are not condemned to a future of celibacy and frustration. Even though full intercourse may not be possible for the moment, your partner may well be able to enjoy all kinds of loveplay which are exciting for both of you and be able to bring you to orgasm through masturbation or oral sex.
- By showing her that you love her and find her desirable, and that you can enjoy sex that doesn't involve penetration, you will help her to relax and build up her self-confidence. This will help sustain the intimacy between you, and make it more likely that intercourse will eventually be possible – and enjoyable – for both of you.

- It is very unlikely that your partner's problem has anything to do with you personally. The cause is almost certainly somewhere in her past life, but if you are prepared to be supportive, you may well be the one who helps her finally to overcome it and enjoy sex for the first time.

Whether or not your partner seeks professional help from a doctor or sex therapist, your willing cooperation in any exercises designed to overcome the difficulties will make all the difference. This could mean attending consultations with her doctor or therapist, and taking part in the self-examination techniques described above.

You will also have to allow for her initial nervousness if she manages to get to the point of trying to have sexual intercourse. Your patience and encouragement will be important to her, and if you both decide to try the sensate focus technique, this will help to reinforce her growing confidence in her own body and sexuality. It is important to keep trying to think positively, and not give up on the hope of ever having sexual intercourse with your partner. The danger is that, out of kindness and a wish not to upset or hurt her, you can adapt to a relationship in which sex features very little or not at all. This is a sad outcome for both of you, and also means your partner has less incentive to try and deal with the difficulty. Gentle persuasion to go for help may eventually get results, although you don't want her to feel under duress because it has to be her decision in the end. Many couples only seek help at the point when they want to start a family, and by then the pattern of no sexual intercourse may have been established over many years. The pity is that you will by then both have missed out on a lot of pleasure because you didn't face up to your problem earlier.

England expects

Over the years, a lot of old wives' tales have grown up around the subject of vaginismus. In the past, it was taken for granted by most people that women only had sex as a duty to their husbands and in order to produce children – desire and satisfaction weren't supposed to come into it at all. Changing attitudes and the research carried out by experts like Kinsey, and Masters and Johnson, have shown that women can and do enjoy sex as much as their partners. As this knowledge has become more widespread, women have started to come forward and seek help with sexual difficulties like vaginismus, no longer content to 'lie back and think of England' as their Victorian counterparts were supposed to do.

Even so, some of the old myths are still around. How many have you heard before?

MYTH: Some women are just too small to take an erect penis inside them.
REALITY: A tiny number of women may have some physical problem, but the vast majority have perfectly normal vaginas that will expand in the right circumstances to accept any penis, however large. After all, the vagina expands enough to allow a baby to pass through it during childbirth and the penis can't compete in size with a baby's head.

MYTH: A man who has sexual intercourse with a woman suffering from vaginismus may get stuck inside her.
REALITY: In fact, the muscular spasms that make it difficult to penetrate the vagina almost never occur once it is inside. The kind of 'penis locking' that sometimes happens with dogs is not

something that you need to be concerned about as it is very rare indeed.

MYTH: A woman who doesn't want sexual intercourse must be frigid or lesbian.
REALITY: While there are obviously some women who are sexually attracted to other women and not to men, and others whose sex drive is not particularly strong, neither of these explanations applies to the majority of women with vaginismus. Most are able to respond sexually to a male partner, and can enjoy sexual intercourse once their difficulties have been identified and tackled.

SEX PHOBIA

While in-depth counselling and treatment are not always needed to help resolve the problem of vaginismus, a relatively small number of women do suffer from a general anxiety about sex. Therapists often refer to this as sex phobia, and proper professional help will be required to try and overcome it. Sometimes, this will be a combination of psychotherapy to uncover the background to the fear, and hypnosis or other methods of helping the person to relax. Many women respond well to a technique known as systematic desensitisation, which has proved highly successful in the alleviation of all kinds of phobias, from fear of spiders to fear of flying and going out into crowded places, such as supermarkets. This involves training in muscle relaxation, followed by a series of exercises in which you are asked to imagine various situations which you find threatening. Usually you'll start with something which produces relatively mild feelings of fear, such as sitting on a sofa with a man who wants to make love to you, then you gradually progress to more frightening scenarios, say when a naked and aroused man is about to penetrate you. With the help of a trained clinical psychologist, you are taught how to relax and overcome the fear so you gradually stop being anxious. This approach is often very successful at helping women whose vaginismus is a result of general panic about all things sexual, but it must be done under the guidance of a properly trained therapist. If you think you might benefit from this type of treatment, ask your doctor to refer you to a behavioural psychologist who specialises in it.

CHAPTER 7

'I'VE GOT A HEADACHE'

Can you honestly say that you've never avoided making love when you knew your partner wanted to? Before you plead not guilty, read through the list of avoidance tactics below. There's more than one way to say 'No':

- Pretending to be asleep when your lover comes to bed.
- Making more fuss about minor symptoms, such as a cold or the proverbial headache, than is really justified.
- Pretending not to notice your partner's subtle advances and concentrating on your book or the TV.
- Suddenly remembering that you have to make a phone call or bolt the back door as your partner is warming up.
- Putting off going to bed at the same time as your partner, 'I'll just finish this then I'll be up.'
- Pretending to have longer, heavier or more painful periods than you really do.
- Neglecting your appearance or personal hygiene so as to put your partner off.
- Criticising your partner and putting them down: 'Your breath smells', 'Your hands are cold', 'You're hurting me', 'Your nails are too long' – the possibilities are endless.

If you still proclaim your innocence, you're either fooling yourself or you're one of the very fortunate few whose libido is always precisely in tune with that of their partner. The fact is that in most relationships, one person's desire is not always matched exactly with the other's for all sorts of reasons.

When it only happens every so often, and if you and your partner are each the one who is sometimes disappointed, then there's nothing to be concerned about. It would be a good sign if you didn't feel you had to resort to any of the devious stratagems listed above when you don't want sex, but were simply able to be honest. Whether it's because you're too tense or too tired, or just not in the mood, it's no crime and no reason for the other person to be hurt or offended if you say so.

Equally, you shouldn't allow yourselves to become concerned if your sex life is relatively low key. A couple who are quite satisfied with having sex once a week, once a month or even less often don't have a problem if they are both genuinely content with this arrangement. It is sometimes hard to avoid getting the impression that everyone else is making love at least once a night and having multiple orgasms whenever they want. For a start, it isn't true, and even if it were, there is no reason to believe that this is the ideal you should aim for. There is no law that says you have to make love more frequently, and you're not abnormal if that isn't what either of you wants.

WHEN IT'S NOT ENOUGH

You could have cause for concern when one of you is much less interested in sex than the other. Of course, there are times when one partner can go off sex temporarily because of circumstances or some particular event in their life. For example, sex may well be the last thing on your mind if you're the mother of a new baby. Even if you don't have stitches or other physical problems, most of your emotional and physical energy is used up responding to the needs of your newborn. What's more, the only thing you're likely to want to do when you are in bed is sleep!

Similarly, anyone who is under great stress at work or having to work extra long hours may have little energy left over for lovemaking for a while. Bereavement, depression or other kinds of ill health may also be responsible for a decline in libido, but provided you both understand the reason and are doing whatever you can to deal with the situation, you can look forward to getting back to normal eventually.

However, if the two of you have always had different needs as far as sex is concerned, or if one of you has lost interest for no obvious reason, you do need to take stock of the situation. In recent years, a loss of interest in sex is one of the most common reasons for people turning to sex therapists for help. Although the majority are women (including some relatively young ones), a considerable number of middle-aged men who have been with the same partner for many years also seek help for this problem.

FOCUS ON YOUR FEELINGS

When one of you is much keener to make love than the other, your relationship could be heading for trouble if you don't try and sort things out. It's tempting to stick your head under the duvet and hope the problem will go away, but chances are that it won't. It may be that the disappointed partner will simply become resigned to the situation and hide his or her frustration, but that won't stop the resentment building up. Worse still, they could turn to someone else to fill the gap. In fact, what often happens is that the situation is just left to fester, and while you may argue and get at each other about everything else, the real problem never comes out into the open. It's much better to admit what's really wrong to each other if you can, because then you can begin to try and work things out between you.

Once you've acknowledged the truth to each other, try the following quiz to help you identify what might be behind your difficulties. The idea is that you each answer the questions separately, then use the answers as a basis for discussion.

QUESTIONS

1 *Do you still fancy your partner?*

2 *Do you ever fancy other people or fantasise about having sex with someone other than your partner?*

3 *In an ideal world, how often would you like to make love?*

4 *How long have you and your partner been together as a couple?*

5 *If you've lost interest in sex, can you pinpoint when it started?*

6 *Have you always felt that your partner would prefer more or less sex than you?*

7 *Do you have a good relationship outside the bedroom?*

8 *Do you want children, and if so, when? If you are already parents, do you want more children?*

9 *On average, how long do your lovemaking sessions last?*

10 *Have you ever had sex anywhere other than in bed? If not, would you like to?*

11 *Is there some change to your usual style of lovemaking that would make a significant difference to your interest?*

When the two of you talk over the answers, try and keep the atmosphere as light and friendly as possible. Make sure you take it in turns to say your piece, and really listen to what each other is saying. It's less likely to degenerate into mutual recrimination if you both start as many sentences as possible with 'I'. The point is to focus on how you feel or what you think, rather than criticising or blaming the other person. So you might say 'I would really like it if we made love more often', or 'I feel upset and rejected when you turn away from me', rather than 'You never seem to be interested' or 'You make me feel like I'm just part of the furniture.' Be as honest as you can when giving your point of view, and try not to go up in the air when your partner says something you don't much like. You're supposed to be using the opportunity to understand one another better so try not to hurt or antagonise your partner.

With luck, your responses to the quiz questions will have helped you to identify the areas that you need to work on. What you can do to improve the situation will depend on what your problem is and its complexity. At one end of the scale, the very fact of opening negotiations may be enough to set you on the path to improvement, while at the other end, you may decide you need professional help to sort out your difficulties.

WHAT YOUR ANSWERS MEAN

1 Do you still fancy your partner?

While familiarity doesn't always breed contempt, it does often make us complacent. Most of us make quite an effort with our appearance when a new relationship begins, and try to show in all kinds of ways that we find the other person attractive. What's more, we tend to keep the less appealing aspects of our personalities in the background to start with – most of us are only too well aware of our shortcomings in this respect. Naturally this slips a bit once you become an established couple, and everyday life together would probably be impossible if it didn't. You can't go on trying to be Ms or Mr Perfect for ever, and it would be unhealthy in any case. You get used to seeing each other unshaven, without make-up, suffering from a hangover or whatever, and you accept this because no one wants to go around all the time dressed up to the nines.

Being 'natural' can go too far, however. Even if you love the inner man, he's not going to seem quite so sexy if he never bothers to shave or shower at weekends, and lives in his oldest gardening trousers and a grubby sweater. Similarly, a man may find it hard to be excited by the sight of his partner slopping round in a baggy dressing gown over greying old underwear, her face streaked with yesterday's make-up. Real people don't look like fashion models, but if you neglect your body completely, don't be surprised if your partner isn't turned on by it.

If your partner tells you that changes of this kind have helped to make him or her find you less desirable, you're bound to feel a bit hurt or upset. Nevertheless, you shouldn't let this stop you asking yourself whether there's some truth in what has been said and whether there is anything you can do about it.

2 Do you ever fancy other people or fantasise about having sex with someone other than your partner?

Your partner may not be too thrilled to discover than you fancy someone else more than him or her, even if only in fantasy. Nevertheless, it's not entirely bad news because it means your sexual responses are still alive and kicking. The point is that most fantasies are just that – if the person in question actually started coming on to you, you'd probably run a mile. Even if you're not convinced about that, you're unlikely ever to be in a position to know for sure. Meanwhile, if your partner can accept your fantasy and incorporate it into your lovemaking, it may do wonders for your enthusiasm for sex. Imagination is one of the greatest sex aids there is, so if your lustful fancies help to turn you on, then you may as well enjoy them for what they are. The main thing is that your partner does not feel threatened by them – you may need to reassure him or her of your love and that you wouldn't actually want to swap them for your fantasy figure even if your imagination does run away with you sometimes. For more on fantasies, see chapter 9.

3 In an ideal world, how often would you like to make love?

When your answers to this question are miles apart, you may have a very real problem. People do genuinely vary in how much sex suits them, so if you're a twice a night man involved with a twice a year woman, either or both of you are going to have to make some major compromises if you want to stay together. Ancient wisdom has it that women are generally less interested in sex than men, and that sex is the price women pay for men's support. Certainly, we're less inclined to accept this today, but nevertheless, there can be an element of truth in it for many couples. Doctors and therapists often hear women say things like 'My husband's very good – he doesn't bother me much these days.' Surveys which ask how people like to spend their leisure time often find that women put knitting, gardening and watching TV ahead of sex, while men are much more likely to put sex at the top of the list. On the other hand, what we might call the 'George and Mildred' syndrome, (well known to fans of the old TV sitcom), has a sound base in reality – a well-established, middle-aged couple in whom the wife's demands are too much for her tired and bored husband.

Where there is, and has always been, a genuine gap of this kind between you as a couple, you may simply have to find your own way of living with your differences. Before you resign yourself to this, however, it's worth considering whether the gap is real and permanent, or whether you could find ways to close it. Usually, this will mean looking for ways to make the less interested partner take more pleasure in lovemaking.

Although genuine sexual incompatibility does exist, it is more common for partners whose libidos matched quite well at first to find that one or other gradually loses interest. Unlike women, who often become more interested in sex as they gain maturity and experience, men are often most enthusiastic in their late teens. After that, libido gradually declines, often falling off most sharply around the ages of 45 to 60.

The good news is that a lack of interest on either side may have more to do with boredom or unimaginative lovemaking than a genuine decline in enthusiasm for sex as such. A woman whose partner understands her need for a bit of romance and who knows that she needs time to become aroused is likely to want more sex than a woman with a less sympathetic partner. Similarly, a man whose partner is happy to try and revive his enthusiasm with a bit of experimentation and novelty may well find that he hasn't altogether lost interest after all. For more on spicing up your sex life, see chapters 8 and 9.

4 How long have you and your partner been together as a couple?

Surveys have shown that the frequency of lovemaking does decline when a couple have been together for many years. Partly this is just that other aspects of your life together take up a lot of your time and energy, whether it's looking after children, work, running the home, your friends and family or whatever. It's also true, though, that the novelty wears off to some extent for the majority of people. This person who once seemed strange and exciting and full of surprises eventually becomes familiar and their responses utterly predictable. Many experts believe that this is a more important aspect for men than it is for women as far as sexual desire is concerned. The theory is that men have a natural taste for exploring pastures new when it comes to sex, and that this is somehow built into their sex drive. After having sex with the same woman over a long period, a man is prone to develop itchy feet, and find himself attracted to the prospect of making love to another woman just because she's someone different. This doesn't necessarily mean that he doesn't still love his partner and want to stay with her, although she's not likely to find this explanation convincing or acceptable. This tendency among males to want to have sex with as many females as possible is the norm with many animals, and is often referred to by researchers in the field as the Coolidge Effect, after a story about the US President. It is said that President and Mrs Coolidge were visiting a government farm, when Mrs Coolidge asked how often a rooster in the chicken run performed his duties towards the hens. 'About a dozen times a day,' was the answer. 'Tell that to the President,' she said. On receiving this information, the President was initially dismayed, then a thought occurred to him. 'Wait a minute,' he said, 'is that always with the same hen?' 'Oh no, Mr President,' came the reply, 'a different one each time.' 'Tell that to Mrs Coolidge,' said the President.

Be this as it may, a woman can still get bored with her partner, even if she doesn't have the excuse of biological programming. She may well find him – and his sexual technique – predictable and increasingly unexciting. What many women say they miss is the element of romance and the feeling that they are being wooed by their partners. Companies advertising everything from chocolates to diamonds, bubble bath to perfume have shown themselves to be well aware of this, and presumably appealing to women's taste for surprise and excitement actually works. While we're on the subject, it's interesting to note the recent TV advertisement in which a woman dumps an unsatisfactory man, choosing to keep nothing from him but the car or the product being promoted, whatever it is. People who make advertisements do their best to keep in tune with consumers' psychology and motivation, and they are well aware that women today are less inclined than they once were to sit back and depend on some man to complete their lives.

Whether it's the male or female partner who has lost interest in sex because of boredom, one way of dealing with it is for either or both to have affairs. 'Open relationships', in which this is accepted, may work for some people, but all too often such arrangements end in tears. Rather than take the risk, you might prefer to concentrate on tackling the problem at source by finding ways to make your love life with your partner more stimulating. For ideas on how to go about this, see the following chapters.

5 If you've lost interest in sex, can you pinpoint when it started?

Sometimes it may be possible to identify a particular event or period of time when you feel that things started to go wrong. Often, a relatively minor incident may mark the beginning of your losing interest in sex, but because it was never talked about or resolved, the problem continues to snowball. Perhaps it was a row in which your partner said something hurtful or something which you haven't been able to forgive or forget. Alternatively, if sex didn't work out on a few occasions, this can set up a psychological barrier to success in the future. It may have happened because the man couldn't get or keep an erection or because the woman wasn't in the mood so lack of lubrication made intercourse painful, but the result is that one or both of you starts to avoid sex to prevent the problem arising again. Once you get out of the way of looking forward to or enjoying lovemaking, it can be hard to recapture the feelings you had before the trouble started.

Both men and women can lose interest in sex at particular times of their lives. The weeks and months after having a baby and the onset of the menopause may be times when making love has less appeal for a woman. Some people have suggested that the hormonal and psychological changes that accompany new motherhood combine to damp down a woman's libido so that she can concentrate all her emotional and physical energy on caring for the baby. Following the menopause, the woman's natural hormone factory shuts down, and this can sometimes interfere with vaginal lubrication, making sexual intercourse painful. Time and a sympathetic partner will usually resolve the first problem, and treatment in the form of hormone replacement therapy (HRT) is available from your doctor for the second. Occasionally, however, such changes can alter a woman's self-image making her feel less desirable, or even that sex is inappropriate now, and such feelings may need to be talked through with the help of a counsellor.

A man approaching later life may sometimes interpret the physical effects of aging as a sign that he's losing his sexual powers, so he avoids intercourse for fear of a poor performance. He needs to be convinced that his problem isn't terminal, and that his enthusiasm and potency can be revived with his partner's cooperation. For more on this, see pages 40–42.

6 Have you always felt that your partner would prefer more or less sex than you?

When the two of you have always had different ideas about how much sex is enough, the reason may be that your needs are simply different. If you really are convinced that nothing can be done to alter this situation, you will simply have to decide between you whether you can live with this. Before you reach that point, however, it is worth asking yourselves whether making sex more attractive and pleasurable for the less interested partner could alter the balance of desire. A man who has not taken into account that his partner takes a lot longer to become sexually aroused than he does may simply not realise that making love has fewer attractions for her than for him. He may be turned on just by seeing his partner naked, whereas she needs a little romance as well as kissing and touching before she becomes sexually excited. Women also respond more to smells (perfumes and pheromones) than men, and a bit more effort put into seducing her may well increase her pleasure in lovemaking. Basically, a man needs to learn what is exciting to his partner, rather than simply assuming that she will automatically be in the mood just because he is.

The reverse situation may be less common, but there are some men who seem to want or enjoy sex less than their partners. As with a woman, it may simply be that a man has a naturally low sex drive, and is genuinely content to make love very rarely. Others, while they will never be the sex maniac type, can be encouraged to take a little more interest if approached in the right way. What does seem to turn such a man off even more is the feeling that his partner is putting constant pressure on him to perform sexually. As we saw earlier, a man is less able than a woman to have sex just because he feels he should or to please someone else. In fact, he is more likely to be unable to achieve or sustain an erection so that sexual intercourse is completely impossible.

On the other hand, a man who is resistant to this kind of pressure may respond quite differently to loving and patient seduction. If you have a partner who has always been slow to warm up sexually, you need to think about what it is that you know he likes. Catering to his taste – whether it be for sexy magazines, silky underwear and stockings or being stimulated in a certain way – may increase his pleasure in sex and so his enthusiasm for it. If you're still short of ideas, you may find some useful suggestions in the next chapters.

7 Do you have a good relationship outside the bedroom?

There are couples who fight like cat and dog and have a great sex life as well, but for most of us, conflict with our partners has its repercussions in the sexual side of our relationships. If you resent the fact that your man spends a couple of nights a week drinking with the boys, you're not likely to be receptive if he comes home smelling of beer and expects you to want to make love. Equally, if you're a man who feels under constant and unreasonable pressure from your partner to do more in the house or see more of family you don't much like, your resentment may make you less inclined to make love to her. It's not unheard of for a person who wants to get back at a partner for whatever reason to use sex as a weapon in domestic warfare, but unfortunately it does nothing to resolve the real issues. The best – and probably the only – way to escape this downward spiral is communication. It makes sense not to let bad feelings spill over into your sexual relationship by talking honestly and as calmly as possible about what's wrong. You need to help your partner to understand what it is about their behaviour that is annoying you, and why. The solution may not be that they will instantly change their ways. A man who enjoys a drink with his friends, for example, won't see why he should give it up, while a woman who thinks her man should do his share of the boring chores, is unlikely to change her mind because he is unwilling.

Compromise is what you will probably have to settle for, and even if you agree to disagree, this is better than silent fury. At least you may be able to promise each other to keep your squabbles out of the bedroom. Making up your mind to try and work things out between you as you go along means your relationship is less likely to be soured by unresolved differences or resentment. And what's good for the relationship between the two of you is also going to be good for your love life. It could be, however, that you feel things have already gone too far for this to be a practical possibility. If you don't think you can tackle the problems by yourself, it's a good idea to get outside help from a counsellor. Organisations such as Relate are quite willing to see one partner alone if necessary, although it is often better if you both go along. Don't assume that a mismatch in sexual desire is necessarily insoluble – resolving conflicts in other areas of your relationship may make a dramatic difference.

8 Do you plan to have children? If so, when? If you are already parents, do you want any more children?

Even in these days of effective and easily available contraception, the prospect of the woman conceiving can influence how a couple feels about sex. When one of you would like to start a family quickly, using contraception which makes this impossible or unlikely may make sex seem rather meaningless. You may even be disinclined to let your partner make love to you if he or she insists that a baby is not on the agenda, for the time being at least. Even if you've already had one or more children, the same may be true. A woman who had a miserable pregnancy or difficult delivery may well choose to avoid sex rather than risk going through all that again. Equally, a man who resents having to share his partner's love and attention with a child will be reluctant to make the situation worse by fathering any more.

The solution here, as so often, is to communicate with your partner. Talk to each other about how you feel, and see whether you can't reach a compromise on planning your family. Unless you can put the focus back on to yourselves and on sex as part of your loving relationship, your difficulties won't go away. Rather, the resentments will continue to fester and make the situation worse still.

At the other end of the spectrum, couples who have fertility problems often find that sex turns into a task to be performed by the clock; that is, when the woman is at her most fertile rather than when the mood takes them. Desire can't always be turned on like a tap, however much you want to make a baby, and concentrating on the procreative aspect certainly takes the spontaneity out of making love. In these circumstances, a sense of humour is an enormous asset, but you'll probably find it hard to see the funny side at times. Don't forget that this is a very common problem and it's worth going for a chat with the doctor who's treating your infertility. He or she will have seen couples in your situation often, and should have some useful advice to help see you through this difficult time.

9 On average, how long do your lovemaking sessions last?

While there's no right answer to this question, it's true that for a woman at least, longer is likely to mean better. When you're in the right mood, a quickie can certainly be exciting and satisfying, but otherwise, too much haste usually means little or no satisfaction for the woman. Instead of discussing this with your partner, and helping him to understand how he can meet your needs as well as his own, you may simply accept that sex is overrated, and not be inclined to bother with it more than you have to. Similarly, if you're a sensitive man who can't help noticing that your partner only has sex to please you, you may stop bothering her as often instead of trying to find ways to arouse her. While making time for a lot more foreplay is a recognised route to greater pleasure for a woman, as a man, you may be surprised – and delighted – to find that turning your partner on increases your own excitement and pleasure, and that your orgasm is all the better for being delayed. And don't forget that, for a woman, foreplay often starts with a romantic gesture of some kind, even before you begin kissing and caressing.

10 Have you ever had sex anywhere other than in bed? If not, would you like to?

Making love at night in bed is seen by some couples as the proper, decent thing to do, and it certainly has its appeal, but there is an endless variety of alternatives. Most animals, for instance, reserve the night for sleeping, and have sex during daylight hours in between eating and all kinds of other activities. Biologically speaking, daytime sex may be more natural. Testosterone, the hormone responsible for our sex drive, rises to a peak early in the morning and falls sharply in the evening, which implies that our urge to make love may be stronger during the day when we are feeling fresh and energetic.

It could be that indulging your private yearning to make love in some unconventional place or perhaps during the day instead of at night will generate the excitement that is missing from your love life at the moment. If your partner has been disappointed recently at your lack of enthusiasm for sex, chances are that he or she will welcome the chance to try something new and revive your interest. You could have a lot of fun discussing possibilities – perhaps you could even make a list and work your way through it!

When it comes to places, the choice on offer is huge. Surveys have shown that the living room, especially on a rug in front of the fire, is many women's favourite alternative, with the bath, woods and fields scoring well too. Men appeared to be a little more adventurous, with many claiming to enjoy sex in the kitchen, on beaches or in the sea as well. Obviously, a bed has the advantage of being warm, comfortable and safe, while the kitchen floor or the bath are harder and more unyielding. Outdoors, there are even more potential hazards, and you need to be wary of the risk of being seen, although some people report that this possibility makes the encounter that bit more exciting.

When you've chosen an alternative venue that appeals to you both, you can build up to the occasion by planning how it will be – maybe the living room lit just by candles, or with an erotic film on the TV, or driving off to a quiet corner of the woods, with a blanket in the car wearing clothes that are easy to get off – and back on again.

11 Is there some change to your usual style of lovemaking that would make a significant difference to your interest?

There is an old joke which sums up this situation rather aptly: 'What's the similarity between lobster thermidor and oral sex?'. Answer: 'You don't get either of them at home.' If so, then that may be a pity on both counts. Often, the reason that one partner gets turned off 'domestic' sex is that it has become routine and fails to fulfil their fantasies in some respect. If you're the one who is feeling 'stale', there may be something specific that you would like to introduce into your sex life with your partner or perhaps you would just like a little more variety in general. Since there are so many possibilities, you will almost certainly have to talk to your partner about what your ideal sex life would consist of as you can't expect him or her to read your thoughts. Some ideas on how to vary your sexual diet without actually trading in your current partner for a new model follow in chapter 8.

CHAPTER 8

VARIETY IS THE SPICE OF SEX

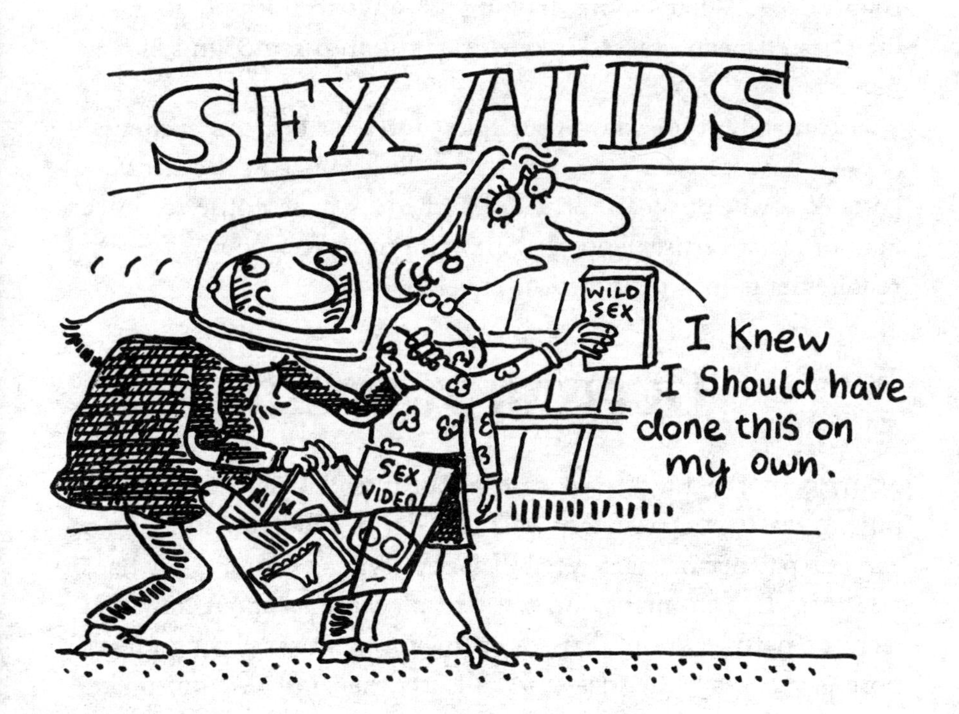

When your partner is the one special person in your life, making love really is just that – a way of showing your feelings and bringing you as close as you can possibly be. Having said that, it would be naive to pretend that love is all you need. Even the closest, most devoted couple may secretly admit that a certain predictability, if not outright boredom, has crept into their sex life after the first flush of excitement has worn off. There is nothing wrong with admitting this. It doesn't mean that your relationship is on the skids or that you love your partner any less than before. What's more, looking for ways to spice up your sex life doesn't mean you're kinky or turning into some kind of pervert.

Fortunately, these days your quest for a bit of extra excitement doesn't have to take you into suspect little shops in the sleazier parts of town, or mean sending off cheques in response to obscure mail order advertisements that promise to deliver your requirements in a plain brown envelope.

GETTING STARTED

Many people feel a bit awkward about introducing the idea of buying sex toys. You might well feel shy of suddenly announcing to your partner of many years 'I fancy trying a vibrator – what do you think?'. You might also want to be cautious about how you let your partner know that sex with him or her is getting rather boring. After all, the idea is to quicken their interest, not make them feel a hopeless failure. What you need is a way of bringing up the subject that doesn't seem too crass or embarrassing. One of the easiest ways to do this is by watching a sexy film together or hiring one on video. It will turn both your thoughts to the subject of sex, and if you choose your film carefully, you should find an appropriate moment to say something like 'That looks like fun – I wonder what it would be like?'

If you have the choice, hiring a video may be the best bet. It is less likely to have the sexiest bits cut out for one thing, and for another, you can watch it when you want – and stop it when you want, too. Most people find watching explicit sex scenes highly arousing, and commercial entertainment films often appeal more to women than pornographic blue movies. For one thing, the production values are higher, with attractive stars often in appealing settings, and the actual picture quality is often better too. What women particularly like, however, is that there is a proper plot with believable characters, which makes it more exciting than a series of disconnected sex scenes with no apparent links or motivation. Men are more easily aroused by purely visual images, whereas, in general, women like to feel involved in the emotions and relationships of the characters as well.

You may well find you want to start kissing and caressing your partner as you become aroused, and some people abandon the film altogether at that point in favour of real-life action. Provided you know that the action on the screen isn't going to move away from the bedroom suddenly, you might like to try making love while you carry on watching. With a rug and cushions on the floor, the woman can lie on her front facing the screen while the man penetrates her from behind, or simply caresses her breasts and vulva while watching the TV. You might even want to follow the action by copying whatever is going on if it excites you – and if it is actually practical.

If the idea of imitating the screen lovers appeals, you could try one of the many sex education videos which are widely available. They show a variety of ways of stimulating a partner, with close-ups demonstrating exactly what to do, and are genuinely educational as well as titillating. With some of them at least, though, you might find that you enjoy the film better with the sound turned down, as the commentary can be rather earnest and didactic, not to mention banal. It's usually clear enough from the pictures what's going on anyway. Even when you don't plan to make love while you're watching, you can use what's happening on the screen to let your partner know what excites you and the tricks or techniques that you'd like to try later. Equally, you can use the opportunity to discover which parts of the film seem to turn your partner on most – knowledge which you can put to good use later. As many of the films will feature sex toys, you can find out what's available, the possibilities they offer and what appeals to you personally.

READ ALL ABOUT IT

As a change from watching TV, you could sample some of the wide range of written and illustrated material on offer – there is everything from sexy magazines aimed at both men and women, to erotic novels and glossy bedside table books. As well as the traditional top shelf men's magazines, featuring close-up photos of impossibly endowed women, there are more serious publications like *Forum* magazine, which include fantasies and readers' personal experiences as well as articles. Incidentally, all these magazines are good places to find sex toys, special clothing, erotic films and such like advertised for sale by post. The 'girlie' magazines tend to have far less appeal to women than to men, and even the soft porn titles aimed at women, such as *For Women* are not to everyone's taste. You'll often find more interesting and informative features in the ordinary women's magazines, which these days include more raunchy articles on sex than you'll see in many of the specialist magazines. If you can't agree on the ideal bedside reading, there is nothing to stop you each choosing the kind that turns you on most and still enjoy the effect together.

When it comes to novels, your choice is enormous. Research has shown that a lot of women find traditional romantic novels sexually arousing, and if you haven't read one lately, you'll be surprised to discover just how explicit many of them are these days when it comes to the bedroom scenes. For something more overtly sexy, you'll find plenty of the so-called 'bonk busters' or 'sex and shopping' novels, the majority of them written by women with other women in mind. Characters and plots are carefully worked out, and the writers generally have either vivid imaginations or interesting lives – or maybe both.

In the same bookshops that sell romantic fiction and bonk busters, you'll usually find a selection of soft porn novels ranged along the top shelf. There are well-known titles, such as *The Story of* O and *Emmanuelle*, together with newer ones published under imprints such as Black Lace. Some of them are reasonably well written, and most incorporate a different sexual variation in every chapter or even, in some cases, on nearly every page. You need to pick and choose among the contents – you won't find all the activities described appealing. The object is clearly to include something to satisfy all tastes, which makes for some unlikely adventures, but it means that you should be sure of finding something to please you in most of them.

As well as your collection of paperbacks for bedtime reading, you could consider splashing out on one of the many hardback sex guides of the kind pioneered by Alex Comfort's *The Joy of Sex*. While all are intended to be informative and educational, most incorporate colour photos and/or line drawings of people making love. These are good for people who respond most easily to visual images, and usually the couples featured are attractive without looking like porn stars with unlikely physical attributes.

Because this type of book is so detailed and explicit, you'd have to be very knowledgeable indeed not to learn something from them, and you could have a lot of fun with the chapters aimed at advanced lovers. Some of the suggested ways of having intercourse are definitely in the double-jointed *Kama Sutra* category, but even when those are beyond you, you'll find lots of more realistic – and exciting – ideas to try.

LET'S PLAY GAMES

The idea of sex aids and sex toys is to increase the pleasure of both partners and simply to make your sex life more fun. Most of them look a bit comical and not all of them suit everyone, but you won't know what you like until you try. You and your partner can pass a few interesting hours mulling over the possibilities, discussing what you'd like to try and anticipating the fun you'll have.

For beginners, it's probably best to go for something simple. One of the most popular sex aids – sold by the million every year – is the vibrator. You can get them powered by batteries or from the mains, but the general consensus is that mains-operated ones are a better buy because they vibrate at a constant speed undimmed by fading batteries. (Don't forget that mains-powered equipment of any kind should never be used in the bath or shower!) Swedish researchers have discovered that the optimum speed of operation is 60 cycles per second, and report that many women don't respond at all to any other speed, so if you choose a battery-operated one, keep some spares handy. The ones sold specifically as sex aids are mostly penis-shaped, and available in a variety of sizes, usually with adjustable speed settings, and may be either simple plastic, or plastic covered with a layer of latex. Some are designed to thrust in and out like a penis, and there's one with a difference which is a small vibrating box you attach to your fingers with rubber rings. It then sends the vibrations via the real flesh of your fingers to the area you're touching. You'll also see vibrators sold as massagers to relieve muscular aches or tension but which some people use as sex aids. Whatever type you choose, you need to experiment with it a bit to find how to make it work best for you. A woman can use one on herself while she's masturbating or while she's making love with her partner or she can get him to use it on her. He may need to watch first, though, because unless you as a man know exactly where and how your partner likes it used, it could be annoying or even painful.

Although some women enjoy having a vibrator inside their vagina, many only like to use it on the vulval area, on or around the clitoris. The only way to find what suits you personally is to try out the various possibilities for yourself. You may discover that, like many other women, you are extremely sensitive in the area between your vagina and your anus, and you may find you're one of those who like to feel the vibrator inside your anus. Remember that you will need to lubricate it – with KY Jelly or Senselle – before trying to insert it, and you may want to use lubricant before inserting it into your vagina unless you have plenty of natural lubrication. Incidentally, you shouldn't put a vibrator in your vagina after it has been in your or your partner's anus without washing it first as there is the risk of transferring bacteria. Some men do enjoy being stimulated with a vibrator too, but in general they are less enthusiastic than women. Even when they don't find a vibrator particularly stimulating elsewhere, a lot of men do get terrific pleasure if it is used around or inside their anus.

If you do enjoy anal sex, you could try out one of the specially designed anal stimulators which can be used by a man or a woman. You'll find pen-shaped ones made of latex or plastic, which can be bought on their own or as an optional extra to be used with an ordinary vibrator. Some have a vibrating mechanism as well. Thai beads are an alternative way of providing anal stimulation – three plastic balls threaded on a string are inserted into the anus then pulled out at the moment of orgasm to heighten sensation. Go gently when using any of these, and use plenty of lubricant to make sure you don't damage the delicate tissues.

Dildos have a long history, but the modern ones are pretty exact imitations of an erect penis. Again, you can choose from a wide range of sizes and, in this case, colours, and they are made of latex-covered foam. Refinements include a built-in vibrator mechanism and a bulb on the end which you squeeze to make it emit fluid as if it were a real penis ejaculating. They come in sizes ranging from average to positively enormous, but for starters it's probably wise to opt for something relatively modest and trade up later if you decide you want to. Like vibrators, they can be used by the woman herself or by her partner, and many men find it very arousing to watch their partner use one on herself. If you are a woman who fantasises about having sex with two men at the same time, you can get an idea of what it would really be like by using a dildo on yourself while giving your partner oral sex.

Boys' toys

The simplest and most widely used are condoms, not just the kind you use for contraception, but ones in rainbow colours, different flavours and with ribbed or textured surfaces designed to provide extra stimulation for the woman during intercourse.

There are several adaptations of this basic idea which can be fun to try, including condoms with flexible plastic attachments on the end, or penile extenders – ones that make the penis feel thicker and longer.

For the couple who want the man to be as hard as possible, a penile ring is worth trying. It fits over the base of the penis and prevents the blood running back out, and can be especially helpful for a man whose erections are limper or less long-lasting than he would like. A refinement that some women like is the latex clitoral stimulator which can be attached to a penile ring. Go carefully when you're trying one for the first time though – your partner may love the sensation of her clitoris being stimulated while you're inside her but she could find it painful, or that it isn't hitting the right spot. You can also get a penile ring with a built-in vibrator. As well as stimulating the clitoris, it's designed to make the shaft of the penis shudder while it is inside the vagina, so increasing sensation for the woman.

One point worth noting is that you'll need to think ahead when you want to use a penile ring – it has to be put on before you become aroused as you can't get it on once you are even partially erect. Similarly, you will have to wait until your erection has completely subsided after making love before you can get the ring off without a struggle.

A somewhat different style of penile ring is one called the Blakoe Ring, which goes round the penis and under the testicles. Tiny metal plates make contact with the skin, and the acid released by the skin sets up a mild electric current. This gadget is supposed to stimulate blood flow in the genitals and increase the levels of male hormones if worn all the time. While there is no real scientific proof that it works, you might like to give it a try.

DRESSING THE PART

You wouldn't automatically think of underwear as a sex aid, but for many couples the right kind can be a terrific turn-on. Interestingly, surveys have shown that red, white, black and pink are considered the most erotic colours by most people, presumably because they mimic the body's natural hues. Once you start thinking about underwear in this way, it can change your whole outlook. Traditionally, black lingerie has been seen as sexy, but lots of men find red equally exciting because the colour suggests that the woman is sexually confident and likely to be a willing and enthusiastic partner. In a different mood, you might like to see your woman reveal simple but sexy white underwear – with all the connotations of virginity and sexual naivety. One thing most men are agreed about is that stockings and suspenders win hands down over the more practical and comfortable tights, especially if the woman keeps them on while making love. In fact, one of the reasons lingerie is exciting is that it is suggestive and sometimes more titillating than total nudity, and both men and women get especially excited by the prospect of making love while she is still wearing some of her underwear. If you want to explore this possibility further, you might like to treat your partner to some of the more unusual items around, such as crotchless panties or a peek-a-boo bra which has strategically positioned holes to let her erect nipples show through. Make sure first, though, that she finds the idea acceptable or your surprise will fall rather flat if she is horrified at the idea of wearing such things or, equally bad, just finds them hilarious.

It's not just men who find lingerie exciting – many women feel sexier wearing provocative underwear, and especially enjoy the sensuous feel of silky materials against their skin. If you're one of them, you can enjoy sharing your pleasure with your partner, perhaps even doing a striptease for him as a new kind of foreplay. Finally, if you decide to try any of the suggestions we've outlined here, don't forget that none of them is meant to be taken too seriously. The idea is to add a little spice and variety to your love life, not to transform you into sexual athletes who are constantly striving to achieve something new. You won't want to open your store of erotica every time you make love in all probability; they're meant to be an enhancement to 'ordinary' sex, rather than a substitute for it. So just relax and enjoy the new elements you find you both like, and forget about any that don't work out.

CHAPTER 9

FANTASIES

The best sex aid in the world is free and yours to make use of whenever you want – your imagination. Most of us have experiences which back this up once we start to think about it. Looking forward to a sexual encounter with someone who attracts you and daydreaming about what you'll do and how you'll feel will make sure you're well and truly turned on by the time the two of you finally get together. Flirting at a party or over a candlelit dinner table, rubbing suntan lotion into your partner's skin on a sundrenched beach or talking on the phone about what you plan to do to each other next time you meet are all familiar ways of enhancing the excitement when the moment of truth finally arrives. And, of course, the opposite is true too. It's difficult to respond enthusiastically to the attentions of the most considerate and skilful lover if you can't stop thinking about your problems at work or how you're going to pay the bills.

The capacity to think ourselves into different situations using our imagination is a particularly human and creative attribute. You can see this quite plainly when you watch children playing – talking to imaginary friends, and turning their beds into space stations or an old dressing gown into a velvet cape. If we're lucky, we never lose that inborn talent for fantasy, but as adults our preoccupations – and therefore the content of our fantasies – are different. That's not to say that all our adult fantasies are about sex, but for the majority of people, eroticism in one form or another is an important, if not dominant, element. This is easier to appreciate when you realise that sexual fantasies come in many guises – night-time imaginings that culminate in orgasm (including wet dreams), memories or imaginary events that are stimulated by something (or someone) that we see or hear. They may relate to the past or to the future or to sexual activities which are exciting as long as they are not acted out in reality.

Not only can they increase our excitement or enjoyment, but they can also be a useful guide to our secret sexual natures, for fantasies derive directly from our instincts and are relatively free of the censorship which polite society imposes on our actual behaviour.

It has been said that 'sex equals friction plus fantasy', and you need both to become sexually aroused. Your imagination will play a larger role when the reality is somewhat lacking for whatever reason. For example, very few people masturbate without fantasising at the same time. The same applies if the person we're actually having sex with is not our ideal partner, which occurs more often than we might care to acknowledge. In these circumstances, we're naturally reluctant to share our fantasies with our partner for obvious reasons. Even when you are perfectly content with your partner, you're still quite likely to find that what's happening in your head is at least as important to your enjoyment of sex as what's happening to your body. What's more, your mental turn-ons will not be exactly the same as anyone else's, whereas physical responses differ much less from one person to another. Your fantasies are unique to you, and tailor-made to meet your needs exactly. Your mental pictures, made up out of memories, desires and basic needs, are brought together and refined over time to maximise their power to excite you.

Your fantasy lover is physically and emotionally perfect – all their imperfections are neatly air-brushed away in your mind. He or she will do anything you want, whenever you want, thinks you're the sexiest and most lovable person in the universe, and never, ever says no. And of course, you only ever make love with him or her in an ideal setting – on a deserted, sunlit seashore or in a luxurious four-poster bed in a château somewhere on the Mediterranean. No one ever passes judgment on anything you choose to do and everything is permitted and free of unpleasant consequences. With such delights on offer, it's amazing that we don't choose to spend even more time in a fantasy world of our own creation.

You can enjoy your fantasy world even more, though, if you don't always go there alone. Before you can take your partner with you, however, you have to say where you are going. In other words, you need to share your fantasies with each other, so you can explore the possibilities together. Before you launch yourself into any revelations, however, spend a little time thinking about how you're going to do it and the possible repercussions. For one thing, unless you are totally convinced that your bond of trust with your partner is rock solid, beware of blurting out something which could upset or disturb them. It's rarely a good idea to confess all about your fantasy sex sessions with a real person as your partner may very naturally feel jealous or threatened. You will probably be better starting at the less extreme end of your fantasy spectrum – making love on a moonlit beach, say, rather than being whipped by a leather clad 'master' or 'mistress' figure. The other aspect worth thinking about is your reasons for wanting to share these kind of secrets with your partner. He or she may well assume that talking about a particular scenario is the first step to acting it out, which is not necessarily the case. You should also ask yourself whether you are also expecting the other person to reciprocate: 'I'll tell you mine if you'll tell me yours.' Some people actually don't want to do this, not because their imaginings are so terrible, but because they are private and sharing them would somehow spoil them. Only you can assess these aspects in relation to your own personal circumstances, but it's worth remembering that you need to tread warily, at least at first, in this highly charged area.

None of this is meant to suggest that you shouldn't share your fantasies. You may have no intention at all of doing anything more than using this kind of talk as a way of enhancing foreplay and arousing yourself and your partner. If you find that you both want to try incorporating some aspects of your fantasies into real-life activities, then why not?

WHAT TURNS YOU ON?

Research has shown that while male and female sexual fantasies do overlap in terms of content, some scenarios are more appealing to men and others to women. Look through our list of some of the more popular scenarios and choose your personal favourites, then compare notes with your partner.

1. *Having sex with someone you love in a romantic outdoor setting.*
2. *Making love with your partner with lots of exciting foreplay, such as passionate kissing, being masturbated and having oral sex.*
3. *Being at an orgy, having sex with lots of different people.*
4. *You're a sexual innocent being seduced by an attractive stranger.*
5. *Making love with someone of the same sex.*
6. *Making love with someone of a different race.*
7. *Having sex in an unusual place, such as on a train, in a plane or in a lift.*
8. *Making love with two people of the opposite sex at the same time.*
9. *Being forced to have sex.*

10 *Having sex with someone who comes to your home for some other reason, say the window cleaner or the Avon lady.*

11 *Having sex wearing something unusual, say rubber or leather, or dressed up as someone else.*

12 *Sex involving whipping, spanking or being tied up.*

UNDERSTANDING YOUR FANTASIES

Although, as we've said, everyone's fantasies are different, research has found some common themes. In general, women's fantasies are more likely to feature their partner, but often transposed to some more exotic setting. Beautiful and romantic locations are (understandably) popular, with moonlit beaches, waterfalls, desert islands and new-mown hay high on many lists. If you're a busy person, with lots of demands on your time and energy, getting away from distractions such as the phone and the family is probably an important element in your idealised love life. Men are far less likely to mention the setting for their fantasy, although quite a lot of men want their partner involved.

Being forced to have sex features in quite a lot of female fantasies, but with all the nasty elements removed. The dream is to be raped by someone you already want – your partner or someone you love but have never been to bed with.

Men are far more likely than women to dream of group sex or sex with two women, sometimes involving being tied down while receiving the loving attentions of two or more naked women. Women who do like the idea of more than one man at a time often involve their partner in the scenario, or sometimes see themselves taking part under compulsion – being abducted by pirates, for example.

Clothes and especially unconventional outfits – like school or nurses' uniforms, as well as the classic suspenders and black stockings – appeal to quite a lot of men. They are also more prone than women to imagine certain physical characteristics, often large breasts, long hair or a particular age in the fantasy partners. As a man, you may be relieved to discover that fewer women were specific in this respect. Wanting some element present such as a large penis or a partner of a particular skin colour is mentioned relatively rarely! Concern about his manner, whether romantic and gentlemanly or self-assured and lusty, was much more central to women. Of course, it may be that the women being questioned were too polite or too well aware of men's delicate sensibilities to tell the whole truth to the researchers!

One of the interesting things about fantasies from the psychologists' point of view is that they reveal aspects of our personalities which are not normally on public view. When it comes to interpreting favourite fantasies, we can see that they do to some extent conform to traditional sexual stereotypes. For example, it seems that the widespread belief that the average woman has elements of passivity and masochism in her make-up contains a dollop of truth. This can be seen in the frequency with which they opt for receiving rather than giving oral sex, for example, being seduced or forced to have sex. Men are prone to reveal vestiges of the caveman approach, preferring to be the active or aggressive partner, and seeing sex in terms of a power game. There is sometimes a competitive component too – seen in fantasies which involve having sex with a woman while her regular partner looks on, restrained in some way from doing anything about the situation, or simply accepting his place as a wimp.

People often assume that sexual fantasies are a substitute for the real thing. In other words, the less sex you're getting, the more active your imagination. The truth is rather more complicated. The conventional wisdom seems to be more applicable to men than to women, at least in the short-term. However, men who are deprived of sex or of female company for long periods seem to lose heart, and their fantasy life diminishes, possibly along with their production of the male hormone testosterone. For women, however, the situation is different. The better their love life, the more vivid their fantasies. It seems that women who are extravert, independent, highly sexed and generally creative tend to have an exciting fantasy life as well. They are also more prone to have affairs with someone other than their partner, probably because they have a yen to experience life and to explore all possibilities. For this kind of woman, fantasies represent a lusty libido rather than a lack of sexual opportunity.

OPENING THE DOOR TO FANTASY

While sharing each other's fantasies can undoubtedly extend the sexual possibilities, a certain amount of tact and thought is usually necessary. As a man, your pleasure in making love to your partner is not likely to be increased when you know she is imagining that it's not you but her boss or Rhett Butler touching her. Many men are inclined to see their partners' fantasies as personally threatening. The implication is that she's using them to make up for his inadequacies and because he is not able to satisfy her. This may or may not be true in reality. Very often, a woman uses fantasy to speed up her arousal and increase its intensity – that way she is better able to keep pace with her partner. Because, as we've seen in chapter 1, women take longer and need more stimulation to become aroused, a man should perhaps see his partner's use of fantasy as a positive thing, because it increases her excitement and pleasure in having sex with him.

As a woman, you might well be shocked or even horrified if you knew what was really going on in your partner's head. He may imagine you giving him oral sex while wearing tarty underwear and fishnet stockings, visualise himself having sex with an inexperienced schoolgirl in uniform or even being involved in sadistic sex games. So, before the two of you venture into mutual revelations, it's worth remembering that some fantasies are just that – imaginary scenes which are exciting only while they are not put into practice. Sometimes trying to act them out proves to be such a letdown that their power to excite you disappears for ever. They simply don't work in real life the way they do in your imagination.

That's not to say, however, that you are better off keeping your fantasies to yourselves. As long as you are both willing to adapt and experiment, there's no reason why you shouldn't trying incorporating each other's fantasies into your lovemaking. When you want to give it a try, start with the list you both went through on page 129, and talk about which of your partner's dreams appeal to you as well. Some are relatively easily turned into reality or lend themselves to a bit of inventive adaptation. For example, if your partner likes the idea of being tied up while you make love to him, you could use silk scarves or stockings to restrain his limbs while you tease and caress him. Unless you're seriously into bondage (see page 145), it's a good idea to keep the knots loose so he can escape if he wants to – it's the illusion of captivity you're after, rather than the reality. Similarly, if you would like to have sex under the stars or play the whore, this is fairly easily arranged. You can use whatever props you like – or just your imagination. If you have a secret rape fantasy, you and your partner can role play, with him the aggressor and you the (apparently) unwilling victim. If you play games that involve any kind of pain (spanking, for example) it is a good idea to have a mutually agreed code word, like 'Basingstoke', for instance, that means 'stop', and can be easily distinguished from playful protests of 'No, please don't hit me any more' that you don't really mean.

When both of you like the idea of sex with a stranger, you can act out the scene, with the man playing the plumber and the woman the inviting housewife, or whatever turns you both on.

It's important that neither of you bullies the other into doing something they don't want to do, or pushes the fantasy too far. On the other hand, an initially reluctant partner might well find that wearing erotic underwear to please her partner or pretending to be a sexually aggressive caveman type is rather more exciting than he or she had expected. For some couples, it's getting over the barriers of convention that's the most difficult obstacle. Once you've started, you can have a lot more fun than you ever realised. Small amounts of alcohol will help to loosen your inhibitions, but remember that too much may be counter-productive by reducing the man's ability to get or keep an erection. You're more likely too to find this kind of sex game exciting rather than comical if you only introduce them once you're already highly aroused. Some of the games you play would probably sound rather silly to an outsider, but that doesn't matter in the slightest provided you're enjoying yourselves. Just because you are adults doesn't mean you're not ever allowed to be silly; it is a great pity if we ever lose the spontaneity of childhood.

You need to tread more carefully when you plan to act out fantasies involving other people besides yourselves. Sex with more than one partner or orgies can be successful, but there are pitfalls for the unwary (see chapter 11). Rather than go that far, you may prefer to keep your games to yourselves, while incorporating elements of your fantasy. For example, you could make love while a sexy video of an orgy is playing on your TV, or watch a video of gay sex or three-in-a-bed rather than trying such scenarios for real.

Instead of making use of technology, you might find it more exciting to invent your own stories and scenarios, rather in the way that children do when they're imagining themselves as outlaws or shopkeepers, for example. You can either make up your own stories from scratch – 'You're the innocent monk and I'm the sultry temptress he can't resist' – or read aloud scenes from erotic books to set the stage. It's been said that everyone has at least one novel inside them, but even if you don't see yourself as a budding author of a best-seller, you could have a lot of fun writing your own mini sex epics. The idea is to fill out your basic fantasy scenario with as much detail as you can – what happens and in what order, the setting, what each is wearing, what they say, and so on. It's up to you whether you use earthy language or wrap up the explicit part in a more romantic way but the point is to make it as sexy as you like. The thing about creating your own bedtime reading in this way is that you can make everything happen precisely as you want it to, and you can press-gang anyone you like into taking part. There's no reason why Jeremy Paxman or Michelle Pfeiffer – or anyone else – shouldn't make a guest appearance in whatever unlikely situations you choose to create for them, and for you. It doesn't matter in the slightest whether you can write well or not. It's the content that counts, so don't be embarrassed to have a go if the idea appeals. Once it's all written down, you can give it to your partner to read or even read it out yourself at a suitable moment. Most people who try this say it's much easier to express themselves fully in writing than it is to do so face-to-face with their partner.

WIDENING YOUR REPERTOIRE

You probably won't feel like doing this kind of thing all the time and the novelty would soon wear off if you did anyway. Save it for when you're both in the mood, and you know you're going to have time and be free from possible interruptions. This is particularly important when you want to go beyond the talking stage and try acting out some scenes for real. You don't want to find yourself opening the door to a visitor dressed in a tart's outfit or wearing a rubber suit!

Playing games every now and then can be great fun, however, and sharing your secret fantasies can bring you closer to your partner. Even when you've been together a long time, you're likely to discover aspects of each other's personalities which have never been revealed before. You can use what you learn about your partner's sexual tastes and preferences to enhance your regular love life too. As a woman, you may be encouraged to initiate lovemaking more often when you know that your partner fantasises about being seduced, whereas a man may come to understand that a lot of foreplay or a touch of aggression increases his partner's excitement and pleasure. Once you've been able to share such forbidden secrets, you and your partner will find it easier to communicate sexually even when you're not playing games. When you've already asked your partner to make love to you dressed as a schoolgirl, you shouldn't have any problems asking her for oral sex or whatever you want at a given moment. Equally, a woman who has confessed to a secret desire to make love to two men at once won't hesitate to ask her partner to masturbate her or try a new position. You'll have discovered a lot more about what turns your partner on and how you can increase your own pleasure as well as your partner's.

CHAPTER 10

AND NOW FOR SOMETHING DIFFERENT . . .

People who fantasise about unorthodox forms of sex usually prefer to keep it a secret. They are afraid of being thought kinky or perverted, and may also be anxious that these labels would in fact be perfectly justified. The truth is, of course, that one person's 'deviation' is another's idea of a good time. As a general rule, more men than women enjoy this kind of exotica, although plenty of women enjoy it too. There are also quite a lot of 'working girls' who make their living catering to unusual sexual tastes. While the prevailing image in society of such people as 'perverts' persists, it's hardly surprising if you prefer to keep your taste for the unorthodox to yourself. But, in reality, you have no reason to feel there is anything wrong with you. You may be part of a minority, but then so are those who enjoy chess or lacemaking. The only 'rules' in this area of your sex life are simple and obvious ones that apply equally to any form of lovemaking.

- It is never acceptable to force another person to participate in any activity against their will.
- You would lose out if you allowed your sexual options to become restricted by your taste for the unorthodox. A man who only wants sex with someone dressed in rubber, for example, would probably have trouble finding a willing partner after a while.
- You need to take precautions if you're indulging in potentially risky practices, such as spanking or bondage. Even a willing 'victim' must be allowed to draw the line where they want without fear that you'll get carried away and go beyond agreed limits.
- It's not healthy to allow this kind of sex to become depersonalised so you don't care who you're having sex

with provided they're dressed in a certain way, for instance.

- By all means explore with your partner possible ways of indulging your taste for the unusual, but be prepared for the fact that she may find the whole idea a total turn-off. In that case, you will have to resign yourself to keeping the unconventional confined to your fantasy life, unless you are prepared to look to someone else for satisfaction.

WHAT'S ON YOUR MENU?

There has been an increasing tendency in recent years to regard unusual sexual preferences not as perversions but rather as 'gourmet' enhancements to the standard sexual fare. In other words, your tastes reflect the fact that you are more discerning, and concerned with more than simply satisfying your natural appetites as easily and quickly as possible. As something of a connoisseur, you realise that the pleasures of love are to be savoured, not devoured, and that subtle rituals and elaborations can add a piquant flavour to the main dish of the day. The idea is to enjoy these 'extras' whenever the mood takes you, but in a spirit of adventure and good humour, rather than out of desperation and shame.

When exploring the possibilities with your partner, remember that there's nothing either good or bad. Rather some will appeal or excite, while others may seem repellent or simply funny. The reasons for your reactions may be buried deep in your psyche, and could well be linked to forgotten episodes from your childhood or adolescence. It doesn't much matter provided you remain in control and keep your sense of proportion.

FUN WITH A FETISH

As a man, you probably have some fetishistic tendencies, even if you've never really given the idea much thought until now. Fetishism can range from a liking for making love to your woman while she's wearing sexy undies to only being truly turned on by some object or material or by a particular part of her body which wouldn't normally be considered erotic. To test whether you have a hidden taste for some particular fetish, look through the list below and see whether you like the idea of incorporating any of them into your sex life.

- High-heeled shoes
- Boots
- Underwear
- Gloves
- Uniforms
- Silk
- Leather
- Rubber
- Fur
- Nappies
- Dummies

As far as a woman's body is concerned, some men are turned on by long hair or feet much more than by what are generally considered more erogenous zones, such as breasts and bottoms.

It's interesting to note in passing that the idea of breasts as erotic would be considered peculiar in some non-Western cultures, where people are inclined to see them more as sources of baby food. And in societies where buttocks are continuously exposed, it is usually only the vulval area concealed with the loincloth that is sexually exciting to men. The tabloids have had a lot of fun in the recent past with tales of famous people indulging in toe-sucking – a harmless enough activity even if the erotic overtones aren't immediately obvious to non-practitioners. Anyone who, inspired by the titillating stories, decided to give it a go will have discovered that the feet are in fact very sensitive because they are so well supplied with nerve-endings. It could well be that, as a result, there are now a lot more foot fetishists around than there used to be. The claims made for the beneficial effects of the so-called 'art of reflexology' by its practitioners probably owe more to the erogenous value of foot manipulation than to the dubious scientific pretext of links to other vital organs.

If you want to try and incorporate your fetish into your real sex life, you're lucky if your taste happens to run to exotic underwear, or some of the more everyday items of clothing, because at least there are few practical obstacles in your way. Your partner may be one of the many women who feels sexier wearing underwear than she does completely naked, and you probably won't have too much trouble persuading her to keep some of it on while you're making love. Perhaps she might even enjoy going through specialist underwear catalogues with you, or be happy to model some of the items you've chosen together as a new kind of exciting foreplay. High-heeled shoes or even boots or gloves might well be acceptable to her, especially when she knows that the sight of her wearing them really turns you on. Silky stockings and gloves conjure up an image of a mature and sophisticated woman, which may be the reason why some men find them especially arousing. Other fabrics, like rubber, silk, leather and fur have a texture which resembles that of skin or hair, and they also have electrostatic properties which can stimulate the skin.

Wearing more unusual outfits, such as rubber or fur, will probably appeal to a smaller number of women, either because they simply don't like the idea or because it just seems too 'unsexy'. Equally, your partner may protest at the idea of making love with you while you're wearing rubber clothing if she dislikes the smell or feel or just finds the whole idea too weird. People (and there are some women among them) who do like rubber seem to enjoy the feeling of it against their skin, together with the tightness and constriction. Some also find the distinctive smell exciting, and of course, as you get more aroused and your body warms up, the smell becomes stronger still. Shiny black seems to be the favourite colour – with its overtones of danger, sin, sadism and pubic hair. Skin-like pink is next in popularity. The thinner kind of rubber clings very close to the body, emphasising its contours and giving a wet look which adds to the arousal factor. You can buy such outfits by mail order, from specialist sex shops and even from some of the more outrageous fashion boutiques. You might be surprised to find that some of the clothes are actually rather attractive and don't make you look like an undersea monster, but that won't help much if your partner just finds the idea of rubber a complete turn-off. If you're lucky enough to be with a woman who is happy to indulge your taste, all well and good. Otherwise, you may simply have to keep it for solo sex sessions when she's not around.

Paradoxically, the fact that fetishistic clothing like rubber, leather and studs is coming progressively into the mainstream of fashion may make it less interesting to fetishists. The association with fun or naughtiness may well contribute to their excitement.

S & M

Uniforms – and sometimes leather, too – are often part of ritual sex games that veer into the area of S & M (or sadism and masochism). What they have in common is that they are about power relationships, which is why S & M fans prefer the term 'slave and master' to 'sadism and masochism'. At the lighter end of the spectrum, many people enjoy sex games of the teacher/pupil, doctor/patient variety, in which the main point is the dressing-up combined with a bit of role-playing to add a little extra spice. A woman who fantasises about being made to have sex and enjoys a submissive role will get just as much pleasure out of this kind of harmless fun as a man. Perhaps more surprising to many people is the fact that even an apparently macho man may love the idea of taking on the role of patient or pupil and being dominated for a while by his partner, suitably dressed up in an appropriate outfit.

You can spend a bit of time assembling your scenario, gathering together the props and costumes to furnish your private theatre, and prolong the action for as long as you want. School, nurse and police uniforms with appropriate hairstyles and equipment all add to the verisimilitude and are quite easy to get hold of. While games like this involve an element of discipline, it is often quite mild, whereas true S & M enthusiasts will want to develop this aspect further. It will usually involve one partner inflicting pain or humiliation on the other, but this doesn't mean that if you want to do this you must be a potential criminal or even a murderer. The majority of S & M fans are quite harmless, normal people who play their games within certain carefully defined limits and never allow themselves to be carried away to such an extent that they ignore signs of real suffering in their partner. The point is as much to give the 'victim' pleasure as it is to please the perpetrator, so going too far would defeat the object of the exercise. The range of roles played in slave and master games is wider, and includes parent/child, rapist/victim, prostitute/client, Nazi/prisoner and Roman/slave. Discipline may be enforced by physical means, using bondage and restriction, humiliation and defilement, spanking and whipping. Ropes, chains, stocks, manacles, whips, canes and chastity belts are likely enforcers.

Your partner may be against taking part in the mistaken belief that she will always be expected to be on the receiving end of any punishment that's going. In reality, male and female participants frequently take it in turns to play the dominant and submissive roles. It may be that more people are attracted to S & M than is generally realised. A study carried out by the American researcher Kinsey some years ago found that 24 per cent of men and 12 per cent of women showed a positive erotic response to stories and fantasies involving S & M. Today, in a more open sexual climate, a similar survey would be likely to produce even higher percentages. While a lot of couples might be willing to add some element of S & M practices to their sexual repertoire, it's probable that masochistic men are in the majority among those who are addicted to S & M. You only have to look at the advertisements in the specialist magazines to be confronted with masses of photos of women dressed like storm troopers, clutching whips and handcuffs, all designed to promote films, vidoes, tapes and phone lines for men who want to be 'disciplined'.

Whatever the truth behind these figures, however, the real point is that for willing partners, any form of S & M can be an enjoyable extension to their sex lives and certainly shouldn't be regarded as forbidden or beyond the pale.

There are a lot of people who, while proclaiming themselves horrified at these kinds of sex games, already enjoy a certain amount of pain in relation to lovemaking – scratching and lovebites are typical examples. Mild spanking is also part of many lovers' bedroom repertoire; both men and women find this pleasurable and it could be something to explore with your partner by way of testing the water as far as S & M activities are concerned. It's even more erotic if your partner masturbates you at the same time. Apart from the psychological factors, spanking may have a more obvious physical effect in that it redistributes the blood supply away from the buttocks towards the genitals, so promoting erection or clitoral excitement.

Games like this may tempt you and your partner to try something a little more dramatic – perhaps using canes or whips. There are various porn magazines for people who enjoy this kind of activity, most of them featuring photos of stern mistresses dressed in leather, with boots and whips ready to chastise and dominate a willing man. The editorial pages feature plenty of readers' contributions, with detailed descriptions of the activities they enjoy and complex fantasy scenarios. It seems to be mostly men who enjoy this kind of severe discipline, and some prefer to be tied down while it's being performed. Being restrained and whipped increases the flow of adrenalin and brings the person who enjoys it to a high level of arousal. Pain also leads the body to produce endorphins (opium-like chemicals), which might account for the pleasure, even ecstasy, that is claimed by some S & M exponents.

Although women who enjoy being whipped or caned are a small minority, mild bondage, or restraint, may be attractive to a greater number of women. Being caressed and teased by your partner and sexually at his mercy is a way of increasing and prolonging excitement. When he does finally 'allow' you to reach orgasm, the sensation is that much more intense for being delayed.

This element of relief from sexual responsibility may be behind much of the pleasure people gain from bondage, suspense and mild pain infliction. By including costume and ritual and surrounding the experience with fantasy, you slow down the sexual action, giving time for your emotional and physical responses to build to new heights.

DRESSES AND DUMMIES

While you as a woman may come to enjoy some of the games and diversions described above, once you've got used to the idea, you will probably find it harder to accept a partner's taste for cross-dressing. It's natural to think that a man who finds wearing women's clothes sexually exciting does so because he would prefer to have sex with another man. Although this is occasionally the case, the majority of transvestites are heterosexual and dressing as a woman is a form of fetishism which adds to their excitement. The trouble is that although this is as harmless as any other fetish, seeing or imagining your partner in women's clothes can completely undermine his sexual appeal as far as you are concerned. Suspecting that this would be the case, many men prefer to conceal or even suppress their inclinations, and it has to be said that this may well be the wisest course. Nevertheless, a minority of women find that they can come to terms with this aspect of their partner's sexuality. Some actually enjoying choosing his clothes, sharing their make-up and helping him to look really good when he is dressed up. A woman who can do this reaps her reward in terms of heightened sexual enjoyment because having her share his pleasure in women's clothes increases his desire to make love to her.

Every couple has to work out their own responses in this situation, and sometimes marital counselling may be needed if the man's tranvestite tastes and his partner's reaction to it are threatening what is basically a good relationship.

For similar reasons, few women are turned on by the idea that their partner finds it sexually arousing to play the role of a baby – wearing nappies and sucking a dummy. For some men, these are seen as fetish objects, while others enjoy being 'disciplined' by a stern mother figure. Sometimes this involves what is often called 'water sports' – a euphemism for urination, and as that is very much a minority taste, it may be best kept to the realms of fantasy unless your partner finds the idea as appealing as you do.

WATCHING ME, WATCHING YOU

We have already seen in chapter 9 that fantasies about making love in front of other people are by no means rare. A more unusual variation on this common theme is the person who finds it exciting to watch their partner having sex with someone else. Readers' letters to sex magazines such as *Forum* often describe the satisfaction derived from setting up such scenarios, although it may be that some of the writers are describing fantasies rather than actual experiences. If literally true, this obviously implies that the men's partners are enjoying expressing their exhibitionist tendencies too, although some writers admit to using rather heavy persuasion to get their partners to agree in the first instance. Friends, neighbours, workmates and even strangers willing to volunteer as the 'third party' seem not to be in short supply, but such trios are obviously fraught with potential hazards. There are the same dangers of destabilising an existing relationship as apply in group sex situations of any kind (see the following chapter) and, in any case, most women are likely to have serious objections to such an arrangement. If you have ever considered acting out such a fantasy, you need to tread very carefully indeed if you decide to try. On the whole, it is probably better to incorporate elements of your fantasy into a pretend situation. You could derive similar satisfaction from watching your partner pleasure herself, perhaps using a vibrator or a dildo, without running any of the risks which are involved in doing it for real. Or alternatively, do it in front of the TV weatherman or newsreader while imagining that he is actually in the room watching you.

When your taste for the slightly unusual is in tune with that of your partner, there is absolutely no reason why you shouldn't enjoy any practice which pleases both of you. You will find information about specialist sex shops and mail order companies which can meet all your needs for props and costumes in the small ads of magazines such as *Forum* and *Connection*, plus articles and fantasies to spice up the fun. While the activities covered in this chapter are not to everyone's taste, there are certainly plenty of people who do enjoy them and the new dimension they bring to their sex lives. Above all, we should resist the common tendency to call everything we ourselves like to do 'normal', and what everybody else does 'perverted'.

CHAPTER 11

ALL TOGETHER NOW

Do you ever fantasise about having sex with more than one person? If so, you are definitely not alone, as group sex scenarios are among the most popular with both sexes. A woman may like the idea of gang bangs, with several men at once, or perhaps sees herself playing the role of a desirable whore, choosing the men she wants and very much in control of the situation. Men frequently fantasise about making love to more than one woman at a time, watching other couples, including all-female pairs, romping together and taking part in mass orgies where anything goes. More men than women report enjoying this type of fantasy, and on the whole they tend to be more enthusiastic about the idea of trying it for real.

There are certainly ways of doing this for couples who want to. Everyone's heard stories of sex parties in respectable suburbs, although finding out who holds them and how you get yourself invited is not always easy or even possible. Nevertheless, couples do manage to find willing participants for shared sex scenarios, either through friends or by advertising for like-minded people in sex magazines. The real question is not how to do it, but whether it's as good an idea as it might seem initially. Before you take even a first step, you and your partner should ask yourselves (and each other) a few serious questions.

What are you looking for in a group encounter?

The truth is that those whose sole object is exciting sex are more likely to come a cropper. Unless the people involved can also relate to one another on other levels as well, and actually enjoy each other's company, there is a good chance that some of them will end up feeling unhappy, exploited or threatened. However, if you are aware of this and try to get round it by finding a couple among your existing circle who want to participate, you could end up with different problems.

For a start, it's not easy finding four people who are sexually compatible, however well they get on socially. Then there's the question of exactly how you manage to move on from your usual joint activities to the new arrangement. You can't just say 'Shall we all stay in tonight and make love instead of going to the pub as usual?'. Get it wrong and you'll lose their friendship as well, but that may happen anyway, even if you get it right.

Is sex with your partner fulfilling?

When you want to involve others in your sex life to make up for what one or both of you feel is missing from your relationship, you could ruin things between you completely. If sex with your partner is already unexciting, you run the risk that you'll find someone else more arousing and making love with them more satisfying. The thrill of success can easily blind you to what is valuable in your existing relationship, so you end up parting instead of trying to put things right between you.

How do you feel about your partner fancying someone else?

You may believe that you're capable of being perfectly adult about this, but many people are surprised at how jealous they feel when their partner actually has sex with another person. Having agreed to the experiment in the first place, it's then difficult to opt out, especially if your partner doesn't have similar reservations. You either have to grit your teeth and pretend everything's OK, or be seen as the uptight spoilsport who is ruining everyone else's harmless fun.

How confident are you about your body?

Anyone who has ever worried that they're too fat, or that their breasts or penis are too small, is likely to have their worries reinforced when they have the opportunity for direct comparison with other people. It's even worse when you can see that your partner is turned on by the new lover because you're bound to think it's because they are better endowed physically than you. In fact, it's more likely to be the sheer novelty that's the real turn-on, rather than any purely physical factor, but you may find it difficult to believe that.

How confident are you about your sexual prowess?

Having sex with a new partner may raise anxiety on this score, especially when the experience doesn't live up to your expectations for some reason. Some men actually find they are impotent in this kind of encounter, while women often find it difficult to relax enough to enjoy themselves.

Has anyone ever suggested that you have a potentially addictive personality?

It might sound absurd, but there are people who have started on the group sex scene just for a little harmless fun, only to find it takes over their lives. It can happen in the same way as it does to people taking up other hobbies, such as golf or bridge, so that it's all they ever think or talk about. Beware of becoming a sex bore!

AN AMERICAN EXPERIMENT

Some years ago in California (where else?), an extended experiment in open sex was conducted at a private estate called

Sandstone. A small group lived in the house and couples could become members for an annual subscription which allowed them to visit whenever they wanted. As well as enjoying meals, conversation, music and general relaxation, people could make love either in the 'ballroom' or anywhere they wished around the pool or in the grounds.

The attitudes and reactions of couples who visited or joined produced some interesting findings. For a start, the men were initially more enthusiastic than their partners about going along to Sandstone for the first time, although some were concerned that their sexual performance would not be up to the required standard. The women were somewhat more reluctant initially, and were inclined to worry that they would feel obliged to have sex with men when they didn't really want to, or that they would be in danger. Both men and women were also concerned that they would be jealous if their partner made love to someone else. In practice, many of them found that this was not so much of a problem as they'd expected, and they found it stimulating rather than worrying. There were also a number of instances where women, having been less keen to start with, quickly became turned on by the experience and began enjoying themselves hugely. Their partners, on the other hand, were rather shocked and panic-stricken at the women's reactions, and lost some of their earlier enthusiasm. This was partly because, once spent, they were inevitably out of action for some time, whereas the women had no such limitation – they could go on having intercourse again and again as often as they liked, if they wanted to. Although sexual involvement between women happened quite often, it was much less frequent between men, and in fact most lovemaking was of a fairly straightforward kind.

For many of the individuals involved, Sandstone seems to have been a rewarding experience, but it is important to realise that this was a carefully controlled scenario where open sex was an important element but certainly not the only purpose. In true California fashion, a lot of emphasis was placed on the way people related to one another, and everyone was encouraged to do their own thing. No one was permitted to exploit or put pressure on anyone else to have sex against their will – in fact many first-timers just watched without even undressing. It has to be said that most group sex scenes are not as carefully structured and controlled as Sandstone, and the disadvantages can easily outweigh the advantages.

All such groups are likely to have their share of sexual predators, whose only aim is to have it off with as many partners in as many combinations as possible, regardless of the feelings of the other people concerned. Pressure may be put on you to join in, whether you really want to or not, and the whole thing can be extremely risky to your current relationship. At so-called 'mate-swapping' parties, large amounts of alcohol are often provided to help loosen any inhibitions. Once all the guests have had plenty to drink, there is often some kind of game organised to get things going, such as the feather and blanket game. This requires everyone to sit in a circle on the floor, each on their own individual blanket. A feather is then blown between them, and when it lands in front of someone, they have to remove an item of clothing. Many drinks and much blowing later, everyone is supposed to end up naked – although the shy can make use of their blanket at this point – and the real fun can begin. Sometimes couples all pair off in the one room, or sometimes there are bedrooms available for those who want a little privacy. Afterwards, you certainly see the neighbours in a different light when you meet them going round the supermarket!

Whether you enjoy this kind of thing depends very much on the individual. You may find that whatever your fantasies, you are not actually one of those who can enjoy sex on a purely recreational basis – it must have some emotional content if it is to work for you. The risks seem to be greater in situations where couples pair off and go in to a different room for sex, rather than all staying together, for we are more prone to feel jealousy if a sexual act involving our partner has taken place behind our back. The ideal situation is when the people involved can take pleasure in just being together, and enjoy any sex which develops naturally out of the circumstances without forcing the pace or feeling they have got to create some sexual action.

The other obvious and serious risk is of acquiring a sexually transmitted disease. Of course, the biggest danger is HIV infection, but there are also a lot of other possibilities which are unpleasant, if not life-threatening. Anyone who is thinking of having sex with someone other than their partner must consider this risk very carefully. Condoms offer some degree of protection, but are not completely foolproof, and in the light of this knowledge, you may well decide to steer clear of such potentially risky behaviour.

YOUR PRIVATE SEX PARTY

On balance, it is probably better and safer all round to express your fantasies of group sex in other ways rather than by turning them into reality. As it seems that one of the main features people find arousing about group sex is watching others making love, you could try imagining you're doing that while watching yourselves in a mirror. If you give your partner oral sex in front of a long mirror, it looks as though you're doing it for more than one person. Alternatively, if you place a mirror at the end of or to one side of the bed, you get the impression that there is another couple making love close by you. This way, you can both see what you're doing from a different angle, which can add to the illusion that you're watching someone else. To reinforce this feeling, some people like to play cassettes featuring the sounds of people having sex which is quite a turn-on for many.

Another way of creating a fantasy group sex scene is by watching a blue film while making love with your partner – you can choose whatever combinations and activities you find exciting from the many such films around. As the Sandstone experiment showed, a lot of people like to watch women making love with each other, or you could even choose a sex orgy film if you want to feel you're taking part in a real crowd scene!

Of course, you don't have to let your imagination do all the work. Sex toys such as vibrators and dildos can enhance the sensation that you're having sex with more than one person. The possibilities are as varied as your inspiration. Either of you can use a vibrator on yourselves or each other. The woman can have the dildo inside her or simulate oral sex with it if she likes. If either of you enjoy anal sex, you can use an anal stimulator too, either on its own for the man or in combination with a vibrator for the woman. When you're being stimulated by or having intercourse with your partner and making creative use of toys like these, it's not difficult to imagine yourself living out your fantasy of group sex. The other bonus is that it's safer and less potentially threatening to your confidence and your relationship than the real thing.

CHAPTER 12

The 10 Top Relationship Problems

When things aren't going well between you and your partner, it's natural to feel that your problems are unique to you as a couple. In fact, many of the difficulties that dog relations between men and women are remarkably similar the world over. What's more, they haven't changed much since the time of the Ancient Greeks – the stresses and tensions endured by the characters in Greek tragedy are much the same as those suffered nightly in the TV soaps.

One explanation lies in the differing natures of men and women which are not greatly affected by where, when or how they were brought up. These differences are almost bound to lead to conflict, and they can't just be wished away or put down to superficial role learning or conditioning.

On top of this basic scenario, individual personality differences between the two of you can arise which have nothing to do with being male or female. Nevertheless, they can be difficult to reconcile. Then you are almost bound to disagree sometimes about aspects of life where you have conflicting interests – like money or housework, for example.

None of these problems is insuperable, but the real difficulties arise if you ignore your differences or allow your disagreements to fester until they begin to undermine your relationship. Before you start to sort things out, however, it helps to have some insight into what is really going wrong between you. Below we look at the 10 most common problems which can disrupt relationships, and suggest how you might try to tackle each one.

1 'IT'S GOOD TO TALK'

SHE: 'He never talks to me – just hides behind his paper or slumps in front of the TV.'

HE: 'She nags me all the time, when all I want is a bit of peace and quiet.'

Failure to communicate is one the reasons most often cited to explain why a relationship has broken down. This is hardly surprising when you consider that a recent survey showed that the average couple only actually talk to each other for 27 minutes a week! The problem is often especially acute when one partner is out at work all day while the other is at home looking after young children. By the evening when they are together, each naturally enough has different needs. The woman, (who is almost always the one who has had no one but children to talk to all day) will be looking for some adult conversation and someone to take an interest in her problems and feelings. On the other hand, a man whose ears have been assaulted all day by colleagues, customers and/or phone calls just wants to relax and give his brain a rest.

The first step towards resolving this conflict is to recognise it as a genuine one without blaming or criticising your partner for having different needs from yours. Then you can begin to negotiate a way round the impasse. One possible compromise might be to institute a 'quiet hour' in the early part of the evening, followed by an evening meal, served at the table with the TV off and newspapers and books banned. This is the time when you can exchange news, discuss your days or anything else which you want or need to talk about. This will require a bit more effort than eating off a tray in front of the TV, but if you can agree to give it a try, you should soon begin to reap the benefits.

Of course, if you try this after the habit of non-communication has been allowed to build up over several years, it's always possible that you may find out that you've actually got nothing much to say to each other any more anyway. Before you accept this, though, it's worth looking back to the start of your relationship. What did you talk about in the early days after you first met? What did you have in common then, and is it still there, even if it's got a bit buried in everyday routine? If both of you are willing to make an effort to understand the other and to try to meet his or her needs, there's a good chance that together you can break through the communication barrier that is blocking your path to a better love life.

2 TALKING TO A BRICK WALL

SHE: 'He never really listens, he just tells me what to do.'
HE: 'She asks what I think, then gets annoyed when I tell her.'

A conversation between a man and a woman may often feel like a dialogue of the deaf, because neither really understands what the other is trying to say. The misunderstandings are frequently caused by the fact that talk serves a different purpose for each of them. As a woman, you probably ring up your female friends regularly, just to keep in touch, even when you've got nothing special to say to them. A man will hardly ever do that, and conversations with his friends will usually focus on work, football or whatever. In other words, they talk about specific subjects, often in a competitive way. They rarely discuss their problems or their intimate feelings, and don't offer one another the same sort of sympathy and support that women give one another as a matter of course. If you and your partner are not aware that you may have different agendas when it comes to conversation, it's hardly surprising if you end up talking at cross purposes. Although these different approaches are to a large extent built into your gender, it's clear that many people manage to get round them by adapting their behaviour in the light of their partner's needs.

While a man's natural reaction may be to offer a pat solution to a problem his partner is going on about, he can learn just to listen and offer sympathy and support instead. Equally, a woman can come to accept the fact that while her friends are happy to agonise for hours about whatever is her current concern, her man is usually less willing or able to do so.

If you agree that you will try to be more honest with one another, you must accept that sometimes this may mean hearing home truths that you don't much like. For example, if a man who's trying to be more open confesses that he does rather fancy your daughter's glamorous young teacher, it's no good going off the deep end unless you want him to clam up again.

3 THE GREEN-EYED MONSTER

SHE: 'I'm sure he's seeing someone else, but he won't talk about it and says I'm imagining things.'
HE: 'Whenever we go out, she flirts with all the men and makes me look a real fool.'

Everyone suffers some degree of jealousy or possessiveness at some time, and in a minority of people it can take extreme forms. Ultimately, it can turn love into hate, and it is estimated that up to 20 per cent of all murders involve a jealous lover. Even when it doesn't go that far, it can create a climate of suspicion which destroys all trust between the two of you and eventually wrecks your relationship. This is why it is important to try and nip the problem in the bud – whether the jealous partner has genuine cause for concern or not. What kind of threat triggers off such feelings will depend in part on whether you are a man or a woman. As a man, you are more likely to be provoked by behaviour which makes you feel inadequate, especially if you fear that your partner is actually having intercourse with another man. This fear is said to have its basis in evolution – a man is biologically programmed to ensure that any children which his partner bears carry his genetic inheritance and not that of some stranger. If you're a woman, however, you may worry more about whether you are losing your partner's love and support – both emotional and material. You're likely to feel especially threatened when you suspect your partner is becoming emotionally involved with another woman, and this may actually be more important than the knowledge that he had a meaningless 'one night stand' with someone else.

You're probably ashamed or embarrassed about admitting that you're suffering from jealousy, but it is important that you do admit it to your partner and, above all, to yourself. However difficult it may be, you also have to realise that accusations and angry outbursts are likely to make the situation worse rather than better, regardless of whether you have real cause to be jealous. It's more constructive to concentrate on making your partner aware of how much you love him or her, because showing your feelings will make you more of a pleasure to be with. It helps too if you can find ways of boosting your self-esteem and confidence. Try listing your good points rather than constantly dwelling on your faults – get a trusted friend to join in if you find it difficult. Some people find taking up some new and enjoyable activity quite a boost – whether it's joining a dance class, learning a foreign language or becoming a governor at your children's school. When you're the one who's on the receiving end of your partner's unreasonable jealousy, tackle the root cause of the problem by making it as clear as you can how much you love him or her. You have to try and boost their self-esteem without reinforcing their possessive behaviour.

4 WHEN CHALK MEETS CHEESE

SHE: 'He's always been keen on politics, and now he wants to stand as a councillor – but the whole thing bores me stiff.'
HE: 'She's always wanting to go out somewhere, meet new people and be sociable, when I'm quite happy staying at home.'

Research shows that the old cliché opposites attract may be true but is usually not the best foundation for a happy and lasting relationship. You are much more likely to stick together if you share certain traits, among the most important being age, ethnic background, religion, politics, physical attractiveness, intelligence, personality type, interests and general outlook on life. To take an obvious example, a person who admires Margaret Thatcher is unlikely to live peaceably with a follower of Tony Benn. The same is generally true when it comes to personality. If you're an introvert who likes a quiet, well-ordered life reading books and visiting museums, you would do better not to pair up with an extreme extravert who loves wild parties and playing rock music at full blast.

Differences tend to matter less when they reflect those you might expect to find anyway between a man and a woman. In other words, when a dominant man is living with a relatively submissive woman, the couple are likely to get on better than if the balance is reversed.

In general, it is true that happy people have happy relationships. That is to say that a person who looks to a relationship to solve all their problems and restore their emotional balance is likely to be disappointed. Erratic and emotionally volatile people, whether they are men or women, will almost always create tensions in any relationship they are involved in.

If you know that your personality clashes with that of your partner, you really have only two basic options. Either you can admit defeat and look for someone new who suits you better, or you can accept the inevitable and find ways to live with your differences. What you can't do is bring about fundamental change in the other person so that they become what you want them to be. This is what many people actually try to do, sometimes suffering years of misery in the process. Believing that the clashes with their partner will go away once they are living together or married, they then wear themselves out in a struggle they can never win. Your best chance of maintaining the relationship – if that is what you decide you want – is to recognise the differences between you and learn to tolerate and accept them. This may well mean that you both need to develop separate interests and activities which satisfy the needs that you don't share with one another.

5 FAMILIARITY BREEDS CONTEMPT

SHE: 'He just takes me for granted, and never takes me out or buys flowers like he used to.'
HE: 'When I first met her, she was lively and good fun, but she's got really mumsy lately.'

You might not find it easy to admit, even to yourself, that you find your partner rather boring these days. It feels disloyal, especially if you still love each other and rub along quite well together most of the time. By now you know each other inside out, and can probably predict fairly accurately what your partner will say or do in most situations. It's likely, too, that you'll have established a daily domestic routine and a social life which tends to be a bit lacking in the surprise factor. Whereas once you made a big effort to please, and were constantly finding out new things about each other, both of you probably try less hard now and tend to take one another for granted.

This problem may well be complicated by the fact that men are to some extent biologically programmed to want a variety of sexual partners. The same is true of bulls and rams – and the reason is an evolutionary one. Males are physically capable of fertilising a lot of females, and over the millenia, natural selection has favoured those who spread their genes around in as many offspring as possible. This doesn't mean that a woman can't be excited by the idea of sex with someone different, but her evolutionary adaptation has encouraged faithfulness and bonding with one reliable partner to support her while she cares for their children. This kind of mutual boredom can be quite a difficult problem to resolve, and sometimes has a strange effect on a couple's sex life. Therapists sometimes find that the real cause of lack of sexual desire for one another or an inability to 'perform' actually stems from what they call 'incest avoidance'. In other words, they have lived together so long and got to know one another so well that their relationship has come to feel more like that of brother and sister rather than lovers, and sex therefore seems inappropriate. If you suspect that something like this may have happened to you, you might need help from a trained therapist to sort it out. Otherwise, there are a number of strategies you can try.

Your aim has to be to create a little excitement and outside stimulation to overcome the staleness. One way of doing this is to organise as many social activities as you can – going out for meals, to the cinema or theatre, going for walks or away for weekends or short holiday breaks. The more you can see of other people the better, as this will introduce the variety which is missing in your lives at the moment. As each of you sees your partner talking and laughing with other people, it will help you to see each other in a new light – or perhaps in a similar way to when you first got to know each other.

6 THE BALANCE OF POWER

SHE: 'I'm really enjoying my new job, but my partner doesn't seem very happy about me doing it.'
HE: 'I loved her as she used to be, but the way she's behaving now really turns me off.'

The changes brought about by feminism have had unfortunate repercussions for some couples. A woman who has learned to feel more in control of her life and to assert herself more than she used to may find that her partner has trouble coping with the change in her. He could be one of those men who feels emasculated in this situation because he has lost what he saw as his dominant role in the relationship. Men's ability to enjoy sex is closely linked to the way they feel about themselves. They need to feel 'on top' and good about themselves because their sexual potency is tied into what might be called their 'social potency'. Once again, this is left-over from caveman days, where male aggression was turned into sexual desire by female submission. Even now, the stereotypical norm is for a man to do the chasing and the woman to allow herself to be caught.

Surveys show that women who accept the traditional

male/female roles tend to have happier relationships than their more feminist sisters. Although it is difficult to sort out cause and effect in this situation, one explanation might be that a woman finds it harder to respect a partner whose male ego has been cut down to size. Changes in the world of work can exacerbate this kind of conflict. While some men are content to stay at home while their partner goes out to work, most feel uncomfortable in this position, especially if they have been made redundant. So, while we may be quite clear in our minds that sexual equality is a good thing, it could take a while before our emotions catch up with our brains in this respect. Some couples choose to overcome this problem by introducing elements of dominance and submission which are absent in their everyday lives into the bedroom. Role-playing sex games, such as teacher/pupil, master/servant or even torturer/victim allow each to take on the traditional role which they do not adopt in normal living. This way of restoring the balance provides the right kind of stimulation and excitement for some couples, but of course it is not to everyone's taste.

7 FACT AND FANTASY

SHE: 'I can't understand why he reads all those girlie mags – they make me feel very uncomfortable.'
HE: 'I do still love her, but I wish she wouldn't keep nagging because I don't fuss around her – we're not 18 anymore.'

As we saw in chapter 9 which looked at common sexual fantasies, men and women tend to differ in the way they see their ideal lover or perfect sex life. This is one reason why you need to tread carefully when you consider sharing your secret fantasy with your partner. If you're lucky, he or she might find yours as exciting as you do, but there is also a risk that it will actually reveal how wide apart your desires really are. As a general rule, our fantasies reflect the basic differences in the way men and women see love and sex. As a man, you're much more likely to focus on the purely physical aspects, visualising yourself making love to gorgeous young women (preferably several at the same time), with large breasts and complete with sexy trimmings such as suspenders, stockings and high heels. If you're a woman, you'll probably be more inclined to focus on a particular man, perhaps even your partner, but otherwise a colleague, film or TV actor or personality. You'll probably go to much more trouble than a man to set the scene, opting for a romantic setting where you allow yourself to be seduced or even overpowered into making love.

As with so many other aspects of relations between men and women, these differences are not so much something we learn, but something which has developed over millions of years of evolution. So there isn't much point in criticising or being upset if your partner's fantasies don't match up with yours as there is little you can do to change things. Instead, it makes more sense to learn to accept that this is the way things are, and try to adapt to one another's needs in whatever way you can. Some couples turn these differences to their advantage by incorporating them into their love lives. For instance, a man may please his partner by playing the romantic for a night, arriving with champagne and flowers, arranging a candlelit dinner followed by a slow seduction scene. On another occasion, the woman may dress as a whore in sexy underwear and high heels, performing a striptease and behaving like the sexual temptress of her partner's dreams.

If you can be tolerant of your partner's fantasies, and occasionally play the role they want you to, then the differences between you can be the key to a more exciting sex life as well as a closer relationship.

8 'LET'S HAVE A BABY'

SHE: 'We've always wanted children, but we can't agree on the right time to start a family.'
HE: 'Sometimes I wish we'd never had the kids – our sex life has gone downhill ever since.'

Traditionally, it was always supposed to be the female partner who came over all broody and tried to convince her man that it was time to have a baby. This does still happen, especially to those women who hear the biological clock ticking and are worried about leaving it too late. And there are still many men who fear that a baby will be a rival for their partner's time and affection, or are worried about whether they can afford to have a child.

These days, however, it's just as likely to be the female partner who wants either to postpone having a family or avoid having one altogether because she is reluctant to make the necessary sacrifices and change a life which she's enjoying the way it is. She may well find herself under increasing pressure to change her mind, not only from her own family and friends, but also from her partner. Interestingly, a recent survey of 2,000 students at Harvard University in America, found more men (92 per cent) than women (84 per cent) wanting children.

Even when you've agreed that you both want children, things don't necessarily go as smoothly as you'd expected once you've actually got them. The man does sometimes feel excluded because his partner seems to want to be a full-time mother and not a lover. He may even go so far as to take up with someone else because he is feeling neglected emotionally and sexually. Conversely, she may resent how much of her time and energy gets taken up with caring for the children, while all her partner does is play with them and take them on pleasant outings. This can quickly develop into full-blown rows when their father undermines his partner's authority by not backing her on matters of discipline.

When such disagreements are still in their early stages, it may be possible to sit down together and talk them through but later on you will probably need help from a trained counsellor. Organisations such as Relate (see the next chapter) are used to dealing with this kind of difficulty, and can explain various techniques which you may find useful in resolving problems of this kind.

9 MONEY MATTERS

SHE: 'He's so mean with the housekeeping, then he complains when I buy a new pair of shoes.'
HE: 'She's got no idea about managing money – she spends it faster than I can earn it.'

While money may be the root of all evil, lack of it is more likely to be responsible for many difficulties within relationships. While the taxman may now be happy to treat the two of you as equal and independent individuals, this seldom reflects the true state of affairs. Usually one partner earns considerably more than the other, and even in couples without children, the man is usually the primary breadwinner.

Regardless of the source of their income, both partners will be just as keen to spend what money there is. The strife often arises when all your money is pooled in a joint account, with no clear rules about who is entitled to spend how much and on what. All too often, you can end up using the money as a weapon, each of you splashing out irresponsibly to hit out at the other. If you don't sort out the root of the problems between you, the spending and resultant recriminations can soon turn into a vicious spiral that destroys your relationship. And anyone who doubts the power of money to cause rancour should see some of the battles waged in the divorce court over who gets what.

There's no question that not having enough money is a miserable experience, but it is only made worse if you row about it instead of supporting one another in your attempts to manage financially. If you can agree to work on the problem together, with help from the bank manager or a debt counsellor if necessary, you can begin to fight your battles on the same side. Some of the techniques used in relationship counselling can be practical ways of handling money disputes too (see page 174).

10 GETTING YOUR OWN WAY

SHE: 'He's always so critical that I end up feeling I'm in the wrong, even when I know I'm not really.'
HE: 'We can't ever have a sensible discussion because she always bursts into tears and flounces out.'

When you're living with someone else, there are bound to be disagreements from time to time, but it's how you deal with them that matters. There are many different approaches, which might include logical argument, losing your temper, shouting the odds, crying, sulking or trying to get round the other person. Some people simply go in for the ostrich approach, refusing to talk about the problem at all or leaving the room at the first sign of trouble. If you've ever gone in for any of these approaches yourself, you'll already know that they are rarely successful at dealing with the real issue, whatever it may be. And when all disputes between you are treated in one of these ways, nothing gets resolved, so resentment and anger just go on building up.

The only real hope is to try to negotiate your way out of the crisis, accepting that compromise will probably be necessary on both sides. Research has shown that many people have no real understanding about what causes conflict between them and their partners, nor why they are unable to sort things out satisfactorily. Usually, they said that their partner behaved badly because that was the kind of person they were, while they explained their own equally bad behaviour simply as a response to unreasonable provocation. It's worth taking a few minutes to consider whether you might ever have been guilty of this kind of self-justification – if so, you're certainly not alone.

The truth is, of course, that there are always (at least) two points of view in any dispute, and if neither of you can see anything but your own, there's not much hope of compromise. However unreasonable you feel that your partner is being, it is essential at least to listen and try to see things from their perspective. It takes two to tango, however, and if you're the one making all the effort while your partner refuses to co-operate, you may need to seek outside help.

How counselling can help

When you and your partner have got beyond the point where you can really talk to each other, you might benefit from what is known as communication training. It is conducted either with individual couples or in a group, and is designed to teach you how to hold direct, open dialogue with your partner, on any subject you need to discuss. The idea is that you learn how to resolve conflicts without putting one another down, and in a positive atmosphere which avoids bitterness and antagonism.

A second technique which can be useful in dealing with specific practical difficulties is called 'contingency contracting'. What this actually means is spelling out, in writing if necessary, what each of you requires the other to do and what you have agreed. It's particularly useful when you're dealing with money problems, or those involving bringing up children, or how you divide the household chores, for example. It may sound a bit legalistic and cold, but it is often surprisingly effective because it breaks the spiral of mutual accusation and recrimination.

CHAPTER 13

If You Want To Know More . . .

FURTHER READING

A great many books are now available to help people learn more about human sexuality, treat their own difficulties and enhance their love lives in general. Among the best of them are:

Alex Comfort: *The Joy of Sex* and *More Joy of Sex* (Mitchell-Beazley)
Paul Brown and Carolyn Faulder: *Treat Yourself to Sex: A Guide for Good Loving* (J M Dent)
Glenn Wilson: *The Personal Touch* (Marshall Cavendish)
David Delvin: *The Good Sex Guide* (Carlton Books)
Helen Kaplan: *How to Overcome Premature Ejaculation* (Brunner/Mazel)
Peter Marsh: *Eye to Eye – Your Relationships and How They Work* (Andromeda Oxford, Sidgwick and Jackson)

Sex instruction manuals are also available in video form. These range from the genuinely informative to the primarily erotic. Either may serve a useful purpose, depending on your particular needs.

If you would like more of a scientific and medical background to sexual problems and their treatment, we recommend:

John Bancroft: *Human Sexuality and its Problems* (Churchill Livingston)
Christopher Fairburn, Mark Dickerson and Judy Greenwood: *Sex Problems and Their Management* (Churchill Livingston)
Helen Kaplan: *The New Sex Therapy* (Balliere Tindall)
William Masters and Virginia Johnson: *Human Sexual Inadequacy* (Little, Brown & Co)

Alan Gregoire and John Pryor: *Impotence: An Integrated Approach to Clinical Practice* (Churchill Livingston)
Martin Cole and Windy Dryden (Eds): *Sex Therapy in Britain* (Open University Press)
Martha Kirkpatrick (Ed): *Women's Sexual Experience: Exploration of the Dark Continent* (Plenum Press)

For scientific analyses of homosexuality and variant sexual preferences:

John Money: *Gay, Straight and In-between* (Oxford University Press)
Simon LeVay: *The Sexual Brain* (MIT Press, Cambridge, Mass.)
Chris Grosselin and Glenn Wilson: *Sexual Variations: Fetishism, Sadomasochism and Transvestism* (Faber & Faber)

For discussions of sexuality in later life:

Alex Comfort: *A Good Age* (Pan)
Tony Gibson: *The Emotional and Sexual Lives of Older People* (Chapman and Hall)
Tony Gibson: *Love, Sex and Power in Later Life* (Freedom Press)

On the menopause:

Gayle Sand: *Is It Hot in Here, or Is It Me? A Personal Look at the Facts, Fallacies and Feelings of the Menopause* (Bloomsbury)
Ada Khan and Linda Hughey Holt: *Menopause: The Best Years of Your Life* (Bloomsbury)

A range of women's fantasies can be found in:
Nancy Friday: *My Secret Garden* (Virago)

Forum magazine is a broadening mixture of sex education

(especially the 'Advisor' section) and erotic fantasies covering a range of variant experience (readers' letters).

WHERE TO GO FOR HELP

Many psychiatrists and general hospitals offer sex therapy. In London, these include the York Clinic, Guy's Hospital, and the Psychosexual Clinic, Maudsley Hospital, but your GP should be able to give you the name of your nearest one (see also below).

A list of approved therapists around Britain (both private and NHS) is available from the Association of Sexual and Marital Therapists, Whitely Wood Clinic, PO Box 62, Sheffield S10 3TL (please enclose a stamped, self-addressed envelope). The British Association for Counselling, 26 Bedford Square, London WC1B 3HU, also publishes a directory of agencies offering therapy, counselling and support for people with psychosexual problems.

Individuals or couples seeking help should ideally approach their GP first and ask for a referral. If this is uncomfortable, Marriage Guidance and Family Planning Agencies are usually able to offer advice (see Relate, below).

On a private basis, help may be obtained from the London Institute for the Study of Human Sexuality, 10 Warwick Road, London SW10 9UG. This organisation offers a complete range of medical services, as well as individual, couple and group counselling with an emphasis on 'humanistic' methods.

In Birmingham, there is the Institute for Sex Education and Research, 40 School Road, Moseley, Birmingham B13 9SN.

SOME OTHER USEFUL ADDRESSES:

Relate
(previously The National Marriage Guidance Council)
Herbert Gray College
Little Church Street
Rugby CV21 3AP
Tel: (01788-573241)
(Couples or individuals are usually seen at local branches)

London branch:
76a New Cavendish Street
London W1
Tel: 0171-580 1087

Directory of Sexual Advisory Services
42 Fulready Road
London E10 6DU

Brook Advisory Centres (central office)
153a East Street
Walworth
London SE17 2DS

Institute of Psychosexual Medicine
Referrals Secretary
10 Peterswood Hill
Ware
Herts

In Australia:

The Australian Association of Sex Educators, Researchers and Therapists (ASSERT)

GPO Box 3712
Sydney
New South Wales 2001

Specialised services:

Sexual and Personal Relationships of the Disabled (SPOD)

49 Brook House
Torrington Place
London WC1

The Outsiders

PO Box 4ZB
London W1A 4ZB
Tel: 0171-837 3559
(A self-help group for people isolated because of physical or mental disability)

Albany Trust

16–18 Stratton Ground
London SW1 2HP
(For gays and sexual minorities.)

Campaign for Homosexuality Equality

PO Box 427
33 King Street
Manchester M60 2EL

Gay Switchboard
Tel: 0171-837 7324
Lesbian Line:
Tel: 0171-251 2942
Text phone: 0171-253 0924

Beaumont Society
BM PO Box 3084
London WC1N 3XX
(For transvestites)

Self-Help Association for Transsexuals (SHAFT)
4 Adelaide Square
Windsor
Berks WI9 9SB

Rape Crisis Centre
PO Box 42
London N6 5BU
Tel: 0171-340 6145

National Association for the Childless
Birmingham Settlement
318 Summer Lane
Birmingham B19 3RL
Tel: 0121-359 4887/2113

Pregnancy Advisory Service
40 Margaret Street
London W9
Tel: 0171-409 0281

Family Planning Association
27–35 Mortimer Street
London W1N 7RJ
Tel: 0171-636 7866

For advice on HIV/AIDS:
Terence Higgins Trust
Tel: 0171-831 0330

Positively Women
Tel: 0171-490 5501

London Lighthouse
Tel: 0171-792 1200

Body Positive
Tel: 0171-835 1045

INDEX